Consumer profiles

Consumer Research and Policy Series
Edited by Gordon Foxall

Consumer Psychology in Behavioural Perspective
Gordon Foxall

Morality and the Market
Consumer pressure for corporate accountability
N. Craig Smith

Innovation and the Network
Wim. G. Biemans

Forthcoming:

Consumer Behaviour in China: Customer Satisfaction and Cultural Values
Oliver Jan

Consumer profiles
An introduction to psychographics

Barrie Gunter and Adrian Furnham

London and New York

First published 1992
by Routledge
11 New Fetter Lane, London EC4P 4EE

Simultaneously published in the USA and Canada
by Routledge
a division of Routledge, Chapman and Hall, Inc.
29 West 35th Street, New York, NY 10001

Typeset in Times by Leaper & Gard Ltd, Bristol
Printed and bound in Great Britain by
Biddles Ltd, Guildford and King's Lynn

British Library Cataloguing in Publication Data

0–415–07534–3

A catalogue reference for this title is available
from the British Library.

Library of Congress Cataloging in Publication Data

0–415–07534–3

Contents

Tables

Figures

Preface

Two unrelated events led us to write this book. The first was market led. Various organisations had, at different times, approached us to advise them on how to segment markets for specific products by behavioural and attitudinal criteria. These were interesting and challenging *ad hoc* projects, yet we felt the need to do this more systematically. The second factor occurred as a result of regular visits to different business school libraries. We kept seeing references to psychographics and 'psychological' segmentation of the market. We began to collect them and eventually read them.

It soon became apparent to us that no comprehensive review of this important but neglected area existed so we decided to do it ourselves. It was an enjoyable task and as a result believe we are now better practitioners of psychographic segmentation. It is our hope that readers will benefit from this analysis in the same way.

Barrie Gunter and Adrian Furnham

1 Introduction: Market segmentation strategies

THE ROLE OF MARKET SEGMENTATION

The world is too large and filled with too many diverse people and organisations for any single marketing mix to satisfy everyone. Unless the product or service is an item such as an unbranded, descriptive-label, universally-required detergent aimed at the mass market, any attempt to satisfy everyone may be doomed to failure. An organisation that decides to operate in some market – whether consumer, industrial, reseller or government – recognises that it normally cannot equally serve all the customers in that market. The customers may be too numerous, widely-scattered and heterogeneous in their buying requirements. Thus, organisations often need to identify the most attractive parts of the market, those they are best suited to serve or that section where competition is weaker or non-existent.

The car manufacturer who decides to produce and market a single model to satisfy everyone will encounter seemingly endless decisions about such variables as the number of doors, type of transmission, colour, styling and engine size. In its attempt to satisfy everyone, a company or business may be forced to compromise in each of the areas it has to cover and, as a result, may discover that it does not satisfy anyone.

The process of dividing the total market into several relatively homogeneous groups with similar product or service interests, based upon such factors as demographic or psychological characteristics, geographic locations or perceived product benefits is called *market segmentation*. Understanding how consumers can be divided up into different types or classes is widely regarded as essential to effective marketing strategy.

Marketers have not always held this view. Traditionally their thinking has passed through three distinct stages:

(a) *Mass marketing*: In mass marketing, the seller mass produces, mass distributes and mass promotes one product to all buyers.
(b) *Product differentiated marketing*: The seller produces two or more products that exhibit different features, styles, quality, sizes and so on.
(c) *Target marketing*: The seller distinguishes among many market segments, selects one or more of these segments and develops products and marketing mixes tailored to each segment.

The philosophy of targeting products and services at specific target groups has gained increasing influence during the post-1945 period. As people have become wealthier and as traditional values have changed, tastes and needs have widened and the structure and requirements in many markets have become more and more differentiated. New products have therefore had to be developed which appeal to particular markets or market segments. It is the function of market research to identify those segments which permit the development of products and services with clear identities but which are, nevertheless, large enough to permit economical production and adequate returns to scale.

Rising real incomes and the move away from traditional class-determined patterns of behaviour will further increase the significance of market segmentation. As we will see in this book, this development will entail the application of more sophisticated techniques of consumer classification based on psychological dimensions, as well as the more effective use and deployment of traditional geographical and demographic criteria to market segmentation. Having said that, there are still instances where direction of marketing effort to the total market for a category of products is justified. For instance, the market may be so small that directing marketing effort to the total market may be the only profitable strategy. In another situation, heavy users may constitute such a considerable portion of the market that the obvious strategy is to concentrate on developing products for, and communicating with, these heavy users. Under different circumstances again, an organisation's product (its brand) may so dominate a market that its appeal is total: it elicits a positive response from all segments of the market and therefore there is little point in concentrating merely on one or two segments.

These considerations aside, however, the whole marketing effort becomes more manageable when some key group is identified as the target market. Products can be developed more efficiently through close attention to a more homogeneous group of potential buyers.

When the group has been identified, marketing communications are often easier and more economical. Costly wastage of advertising expenditure (e.g., due to overlapping groups with neither the means nor the intention to buy) can be avoided.

Today's companies are finding it increasingly hard to practise mass marketing and in any case, mass markets are undergoing 'demystification'. Consumers will soon be able to enjoy a multiplicity of television channels supplied by terrestrial, satellite and cable distribution systems in addition to the numerous radio stations, magazines and newspapers to which they are exposed. In future, advertisers will be forced to design products that fit with the multiplicity of channels, with multiple retail outlets and with a multiplicity of discrete consumer target audiences. The necessity of subtle, sensitive target marketing has now received almost total recognition.

TARGET MARKETING

Companies are increasingly embracing target marketing. Target marketing helps sellers identify marketing opportunities more successfully. The marketers can develop the 'right' product for each target market. They can adjust their prices, distribution channels and advertising to reach the target market efficiently. Instead of scattering their marketing effort ('shotgun' approach) they can focus it on the buyers who have the greatest purchase interest ('rifle' approach).

Target marketing calls for three steps:

(a) *Market segmentation*: The act of dividing a market into distinct groups of buyers who might require separate products and/or marketing mixes. The company identifies different ways to segment the market and develops profiles of the resulting market segments.
(b) *Market targeting*: The act of evaluating and selecting one or more of the market segments to enter.
(c) *Product positioning*: The act of formulating a competitive positioning for the product and a detailed marketing mix.

SEGMENTING CONSUMER MARKETS

Market segmentation results from a determination of factors that distinguish a certain group of consumers from the overall market. Classifying consumers in this way can help manufacturers and communicators to adjust their advertising, marketing, distribution

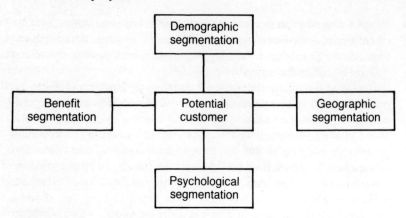

Figure 1.1 Marketing segmentation bases

channels and prices to reach target markets more effectively. Understanding the physical characteristics of consumers in terms of age, sex, geographic location, income and expenditure patterns, mobility and their psychological characteristics covering activity patterns and attitudes, interests and values, is central to the success of the overall marketing strategy.

There are four commonly used bases for segmenting consumer markets (see Figure 1.1). The first two can be broadly subsumed under *Physical Attribute Classification* and the others represent forms of *Behavioural or Psychological Attribute Classification.*

Physical Attribute Classification includes: (i) *geographic segmentation*, which refers to the dividing of an overall market into homogeneous groups on the basis of population location and has been used for hundreds of years; and (ii) *demographic segmentation*, which refers to the dividing of an overall market into homogeneous groups based upon characteristics such as age, sex and income level. Demographic segmentation is the most commonly used method of subdividing total markets.

Behavioural Attribute Classification, on the other hand, includes, (i) *Product use and benefit segmentation* which focuses upon product purchase behaviour and the benefits the consumer expects to derive from a product or service. These segmentation bases can be important to marketing strategies, provided they are significantly related to differences in buying behaviour; and (ii) *psychological segmentation*, which utilises profiles of consumers developed either from standardised personality inventories or from analyses of the reported activities, opinions, interests and lifestyles of individuals.

As we will explain in this first chapter, marketing researchers have traditionally used demographic and socio-economic data to develop market segments and predict the market behaviour of individuals. Growing disenchantment with such segmentation schemes, initially witnessed within the business community in the United States (and later spreading to other national and international markets), led to the investigation of alternatives.

One such alternative was the concept of the life cycle. This line of exploration revealed that for various sets of products and services, a household's life-cycle stage (or development) is a better predictor of ownership or use than straight demographics alone (Wells and Gubar, 1966).

Even life-cycle data, however, cannot explain why two households with identical demographic profiles can exhibit radically different behaviour in the marketplace. To this end, researchers have examined the role of various lifestyle variables in the marketing mix. These variables, which variously comprise standardised, classical personality measures, or custom-built, consumer-oriented psychological inventories, have been explored in a wide range of marketing contexts. This book will provide an extensive review and critique of the work that has been done in this field.

PHYSICAL ATTRIBUTE CLASSIFICATION

Geographic segmentation

This approach divides the market into different geographic units like regions, counties, states, cities, neighbourhoods and TV regions. For some countries and territories there are enormous and quite specific differences which exist. These segments are important because where people live, work and play can have a great impact on their purchasing behaviour.

There is no single best method for geographically segmenting one market. Major geographic segmentation dimensions can be grouped into two categories: *market scope factors* and *geographic market measures*. Market scope factors distinguish between global, national, regional and local markets. Geographic market measures can include such factors as population density (urban, suburban, rural), climate (cold, temperate, tropical, etc.), standardised market areas and census classifications.

All sorts of geographic factors can make a substantial difference in consumer purchasing because geographic regions differ in climate,

Table 1.1: CACI market analysis geodemographic classifications

Classification	Characteristics	Percentage of 1984 UK households
A Agricultural areas	1 Agricultural villages 2 Areas of farms and small holdings	3.3
B Modern family housing higher incomes	3 Cheap modern private housing 4 Recent private housing, young families 5 Modern private housing, older children 6 New detached houses, young families 7 Military bases	15.3
C Older housing of intermediate status	8 Mixed owner-occupied and council estate 9 Small town centres and flats above shops 10 Villages with non-farm employment 11 Older private housing, skilled workers	18.6
D Poor quality older terraced housing	12 Unimproved terraced with older housing 13 Pre-1914 terraces low income families 14 Tenement flats lacking amenities	4.5
E Better-off council estates	15 Council estates, well-off older workers 16 Recent council estates 17 Council estates, well-off young workers 18 Small council houses often Scottish	12.3
F Less well-off council estates	19 Low rise estates in industrial towns 20 Inter-war council estates, older people 21 Council housing for the elderly	10.2
G Poorest council estates	22 New council estates in inner cities 23 Overspill estates high unemployment 24 Council estates with overcrowding 25 Council estates with worst poverty	6.7
H Multi-racial areas	26 Multi-occupied terraces poor Asians	3.4

		27	Owner-occupied terraces with Asians	
		28	Multi-let housing with Afro-Caribbeans	
		29	Better-off multi-ethnic areas	
I	High status non-family areas	30	High status areas few children	4.8
		31	Multi-let big old houses and flats	
		32	Furnished flats mostly single people	
J	Affluent suburban housing	33	Inter-war semis white collar workers	15.9
		34	Spacious inter-war semis big gardens	
		35	Villages with wealthy older commuters	
		36	Detached houses exclusive suburbs	
K	Better-off retirement areas	37	Private houses, well-off elderly	4.8
		38	Private flats with single pensioners	

Source: Whitehead, R.T., 'Geodemographics – the bridge between conventional demographics and lifestyles', *Admap*, May 1987, 23–6.

cultural groups that have settled there, time zones and so on. But with increasing mobility and universal telecommunications, distinct geographically-based market segments are disappearing.

The above classifications provide a basic framework of the most common dimensions upon which geographic market decisions can be based. The categories are not mutually exclusive however. Within some classifications, more than one variable should be examined, and several forms of geographic bases should be explored and analysed to maximise the value of the marketing information.

To maximise the value of the physical dimensions, a composite geodemographic model has been used for segmentation analysis. The basic premise behind geodemographics is that the sum of the whole is more powerful than the individual parts (geography, demographics and socio-economic factors). Essentially, geodemographics consists of neighbourhood classifications. Consumers are classified principally on the basis of where they live, in a comparable fashion to the way social class defines consumers by their occupation. Both social class and type of residential neighbourhood can provide useful breaks according to which consumer behaviour can be classified and predicted.

There is now plenty of choice of geodemographic systems. In the United Kingdom, they each take 1981 census statistics to classify the small neighbourhoods by which the census is reported. An area of posh suburbia or grotty council housing cannot escape from its basic character, however sophisticated the statistical techniques or however detailed the way it is described. The best known and most widely accepted is the ACORN system, which stands for A Classification of Residential Neighbourhoods. Others include Pinpoint's PIN classification, CCN's MOSAIC and McIntyre's Superprofiles.

ACORN takes account of the socio-economic structure and family structure of a neighbourhood and by relating these variables to different types of residential areas can also usefully say something about lifestyle. Table 1.1 shows how the 11 ACORN groups are broadly defined and how the 38 different types of area are divided between them.

MOSAIC adds personal financial data to the mix, which contributes little of value to most general marketing applications. PIN has developed extraordinarily detailed geographic precision which again offers little extra for most applications. The census is only reported for broad neighbourhoods, not individual homes, and in so far as discrete communities do exist on the ground, the hundred metre resolution used by other systems is quite adequate to locate them.

Neighbourhood classifications have been found to reveal more about lifestyles than traditional standard demographics. One of ACORN's first claims to offer new insights in market segmentation was that it described the differences between the readerships of individual quality press bibles whose profiles appeared similar in terms of traditional demographics. If we take a single socio-economic division, for instance that of CI, ACORN could provide further distinctions between owner-occupied neighbourhoods, areas of better-off council housing and areas of poor council housing. ACORN has also been found to relate well to formal lifestyle classifications, on which this book focuses its attention.

Demographic and socio-economic segmentation

Demography is the statistical study of human populations and their vital characteristics. Socio-economic factors, which are closely linked to demographics, are used to analyse a population in terms of economic and social classes. The broad definition of demographics as used in market analysis typically includes both demographic and socio-economic variables.

The most common approach to market segmentation is to divide consumer groups according to demographic variables. These variables – age, sex, income, occupation, education, household size and stage in the family life cycle – among others are typically used to identify market segments and to develop appropriate marketing mixes. Demographic variables are often used in market segmentation for three reasons:

(a) They are easy to identify and measure.
(b) They are associated with the sale of many products and services.
(c) They are typically referred to in describing the audiences of advertising media, so that media buyers and others can easily pinpoint a desired target market.

Vast quantities of data are available to assist the marketing planner in segmenting markets on a demographic basis. Sex is an obvious variable for segmenting markets because many products are sex-specific. Household size data can be of special use to their businesses. Age, household size, family life-cycle stage and income and expenditure patterns are important factors in determining purchase patterns. The distinct differences based upon demographic factors justify their frequent use as a basis for segmentation. Many of the common demographic dimensions are interrelated, or similar, from an analytical perspective. Recognising this, it is possible to group these variables into four major categories. Since demographic analysis has been the traditional approach to market segmentation, and these dimensions are understood by most marketers, comments about these categories will be kept brief.

Market size factors

This group consists of population statistics; the number of households or families, and household or family size. The key variable that must be gathered in a demographic study is the total population of the market in question. Although total population is not a segmenting variable (since rarely is it feasible to go after the whole market), it acts as a comparative yardstick upon which other dimensions can be evaluated.

The number of households or families in an area provides a similar measure. However, instead of determining how many individuals are within a given market, the number of 'buying centres' are identified. The third variable within this group, household or family size, is a derivation of the other two. By dividing the number of households or families into the total population, the average household or family size for an area can easily be calculated.

Splitting the market demographically

Marketing planners can divide markets according to a variety of objective, physical attribute criteria based on demographic information obtained from consumers. Such variables include gender, age, ethnic origin, nationality, religion and marital status. Used singly, however, these demographic forms of consumer classification may provide insufficiently sensitive or insightful indications about relevant market character and movements for many product markets. For instance, while marital status may be an important variable for many marketers, its significance changes with the times. Due to changing lifestyles, including women returning to work and pursuing careers, high divorce rates, increases in single-parent families and cohabitation, marital status can take on a different meaning, and indeed has become a more significant variable for many markets providing a more representative profile of potential customers.

Examining the numbers of males and females in a market has been and remains important, but once again, this division has taken on changing significance. While there are still many male or female oriented products or services in the marketplace, many changes have occurred in purchasing behaviour. A lot of this is due to the redefinition of traditional male–female roles that has taken place as increased numbers of women have entered the workforce.

Age and life stage

Age has long been recognised by marketers as an important factor underlying many purchasing behaviours. Demands for various goods and commodities change with age. Needs and preferences change as people get older. Age, however, means more than simply how old a person is. A more subtle variable than chronological age in the marketing context is the life stage a person has reached. This is defined by a group of demographic and other factors which together can produce a comprehensive profile of the consumer and the particular commodities to which high priority is assigned.

Life cycle and life stage represent two more sophisticated ways of classifying consumers than simple demographics. Family life cycle, for instance, is a construct which has been popular in consumer expenditure research for several decades (e.g., Arndt, 1974; Lansing and Morgan, 1955; Wells and Gubar, 1966). A set of composite variables, family life cycle combines trends in income and family composition with changes in demands placed on income. The family life cycle is the process of family formation and dissolution. Using this concept, the marketing planner combines the family characteristics of age, marital status, number and ages of children and level of income to develop a marketing strategy.

According to its proponents, different life-cycle stages are associated with distinct behavioural characteristics and buying patterns. Young singles, for example, have relatively few financial burdens and tend to be purchasers of new fashion items; they are recreation-oriented and make purchase of basic kitchen equipment, cars and holidays. By contrast, young marrieds tend to be heavy purchasers of baby products, homes, television sets, toys, and washers and dryers. Their liquid assets tend to be relatively low, and they are more likely to have disposable income; more time for recreation, self-education and travel, and more than one member in the work force than their full-nest counterparts with younger children in other stages of the family life cycle.

Analysis of life-cycle stages often gives better results than reliance upon single variables, such as age. For example, the buying patterns of a 25-year-old single man are very different to those of a father of the same age. The family of five, headed by parents in their forties, is a more likely prospect for the World Book Encyclopaedia than the 40-year-old divorced person with no children.

Family life-cycle variables have been used to study a wide range of family financial characteristics and expenditure patterns. Lansing and Morgan (1955) studied income and assets as well as expenditures for housing and durables using a seven-stage family life-cycle model based on the age and marital status of the household head and the age of the youngest child. The pattern of income over family life cycle followed an inverted U-shape. Income increased over the life cycle, peaking when there were dependent children in the family. As the children left home, income decreased until the household head retired.

Wells and Gubar (1966) expanded the Lansing and Morgan family life cycle to include the employment or retirement of the household head. This compound family life-cycle variable was found to be more effective than simply knowing the age of the head of household in predicting expenditures for food, durables, housing and holidays. In a further secondary analysis of a different dataset, however, the same researchers found age was superior to family life cycle in predicting expenditure for selected clothing items, which were more age-related.

One criticism of the above research is that the family life-cycle variable used by Wells and Gubar focused on a traditional family set-up, while non-traditional families were excluded. Murphy and Staples

(1979) offered an updated family life-cycle classification taking into account important changes in family structures that had occurred over the years. This modernised model of family life cycle comprised 13 stages. Even this model omitted cohabiting couples, never-married individuals with children, married couples who were separated, and young and middle-aged widows and widowers.

Despite its popularity, the family life cycle has been criticised. Ferber (1979) has argued that when socio-economic and demographic variables – especially income – are controlled, family life-cycle variables may have little effect on expenditures. Other critics (Murphy and Staples, 1979; Frost, 1969) have suggested that the effect of family composition is obscured by family life-cycle variables. As yet, there is no empirical evidence to support or refute these contentions.

The well documented incidences of divorce, postponement of marriage and childbearing and voluntary childlessness have resulted in an increase in the number of families who are excluded from traditional family life-cycle categories. As a result, there has been controversy in the consumer behaviour literature over the appropriate definition of the family life cycle.

Consumer expenditure research involving family life-cycle variables has been criticised for three reasons. First, alternative definitions have not been tested over a comprehensive range of goods and services (Ferber, 1979). Recent studies have been designed to correct this inadequacy. Fritzsche (1981), for example, compared expenditures for energy over the family life cycle using modified versions of both the Wells and Gubar (1966) and Murphy and Staples (1979) models. The Wells and Gubar model was modified by the addition of a stage called the Mature Nest, which included households with more than two adults, but no children under the age of 18; the Murphy and Staples model was modified by the inclusion of never-married and prematurely widowed parents. Expenditure for energy was found to vary across different stages of the cycle, though the two models themselves were not compared. Derrick and Lehfield (1980) proposed a simplified version of the family life cycle, in which family life-cycle variables were treated individually. They compared two models in predicting expenditures for food: a model that included the family life-cycle variables used by Wells and Gubar (1966) and a model that included the individual variables used to define family life cycle (age and marital status of the household head and age of the youngest child). There was a slight improvement in predictive ability when these variables were treated individually.

Consumer researchers have proposed increasing the number of

family life-cycle stages in order to accommodate non-traditional family groups, such as single-parent families and married couples who choose not to bear children (Gilly and Enis, 1982; Murphy and Staples, 1979; Stampfl, 1978). Such revisions presuppose that increasing the number of family life-cycle stages would be useful in predicting family expenditures for goods and services. Wagner and Hanna (1983) tested the effectiveness of the traditional family life cycle, the revised family life cycle and family composition variables in models predicting total family clothing expenditures. They found little difference in the predictability of the three sets of variables. Even in models controlling for socio-economic and demographic variables, family life-cycle and family composition variables had little predictive ability, independent of income.

SAGACITY

Sagacity is a system of consumer groupings introduced by UK market research agency, Research Services Ltd. According to this organisation, a classification system should ideally combine both descriptive features and predictive power. Thus, direct classifiers based, for instance, on product usage, though superficially very attractive, have only a limited general utility. In other words, such information can be used as a classification system for a particular product, but it will have no predictive value for other products unless they are closely related to that particular product.

Demographic characteristics such as age and social grade may now have lost much of their previous discriminating power due to profound changes in society, and also because they are often used as a single dimension. Cornish (1981) argued that when interlaced with other data, particularly that relating to life cycle and income level, this can produce highly discriminated population segments without abandoning the valuable role social grade has for many markets and media.

The fundamental basis for Sagacity groups is that people have different aspirations and behaviour patterns as they move through their life cycle. Four main stages of the life cycle constitute the framework:

Total Adults 15+ (100%)

| The dependent stage (16%) | The pre-family stage (8%) | The family stage (36%) | The later stage (40%) |

The second and third levels of the groupings are related to the income and occupational characteristics of the individual or couple forming the household. The income breakdown is applied only at the family stage and the later stage, because of the relatively small sample sizes of the other two groups (the dependent stage and pre-family stage), which makes subdivision unrealistic. Also, differences in disposable income are less marked and therefore less important in these earlier stages.

A 12-cell segmentation of the adult population is produced by this approach and Sagacity is often applied to the male and female populations separately.

SAGACITY GROUPINGS

Dependant, White (DW) 6 per cent
Mainly under 24s, living at home or full-time student, where head of household is in an ABC1 occupation group.

Dependant, Blue (DB) 9 per cent
Mainly under 24s, living at home or full-time student, where head of household is in a C2DE occupation group.

Pre-family, White (PFW) 4 per cent
Under 35s who have established their own household but have no children and where the head of household is in an ABC1 occupation group.

Pre-family, Blue (PFB) 4 per cent
Under 35s who have established their own household but have no children and where the head of household is in a C2DE occupation group.

Family, Better-off, White (FW+) 6 per cent
Housewives and heads of household, under 65, with one or more children in the household, in the 'better-off' income group and where the head of household is in an ABC1 occupation group (65 per cent are AB).

Family, Better-off, Blue (FB+) 9 per cent
Housewives and heads of household, under 65, with one or more children in the household, in the 'better-off' income group and where the head of household is in a C2DE occupation group (72 per cent are C2).

Family, Worse-off, White (FW−) 8 per cent
Housewives and heads of household, under 65, with one or more children in the household, in the 'worse-off' income group and where the head of household is in an ABC1 occupation group (72 per cent are C1).

Family, Worse-off, Blue (FB−) 14 per cent
Housewives and heads of household, under 65, with one or more children in the household, in the 'worse-off' income group and where the head of household is in a C2DE occupation group (47 per cent are DE).

Late, Better-off, White (LW+) 5 per cent
Includes all adults whose children have left home or who are over 35 and childless, are in the 'better-off' income group and where the head of household is in an ABC1 occupation group (60 per cent are AB).

Late, Better-off, Blue (LB+) 7 per cent
Includes all adults whose children have left home or who are over 35 and childless, are in the 'better-off' income group and where the head of household is in a C2DE occupation group (69 per cent are C2).

Late, Worse-off, White (LW−) 9 per cent
Includes all adults whose children have left home or who are over 35 and childless, are in the 'worse-off' income group and where the head of household is in an ABC1 occupation group (71 per cent are C1).

Late, Worse-off, Blue (LB−) 19 per cent
Includes all adults whose children have left home or who are over 35 and childless, are in the 'worse-off' income group and where the head of household is in a C2DE occupation group (70 per cent are DE).

Life stage and stress

Recently a psychological dimension has been added to the consideration of life-cycle classification of markets. Changes in life status which occur on moving through the life cycle may also bring changes in lifestyle. Such changes can bring stresses to bear upon household members. A status change, whether for good or bad, can have unsettling effects which can be of a profound psychological nature. A rapidly growing body of empirical research has established that changes in status can lead to serious physical and emotional problems for some individuals. Life changes can lead to stress which produces disorientation and the onset of physical disease. The extent of these effects has been found to be proportional to the amount of stress experienced.

What effects can stress have upon consumer behaviour? Elevated stress may lead to increased dissatisfaction with life in general and with product and service choices in particular, and this can lead to changes in consumption behaviour. On the other hand, consumers under stress may simply decline to change, clinging to present patterns as a means of coping with the chaos in their lives. Finally, by upsetting consumers, stress may make them more ready to entertain the suggestions of others, including marketers. This influence can, of course, be for better or worse; the stressed consumer could be encouraged to adopt more desirable practices, or he/she could be manipulated into making a number of hasty purchases and taking actions they will regret when stress levels have receded.

Andreason (1984) examined changes in consumer life status and their effects on brand preferences and overall satisfaction with products and services purchased. Lifestyle changes can result in significant shifts in household priorities and product preferences. As priorities change so too do needs. Significant changes include changes of job, promotion within a job, having children and losing family members through death, divorce and separation.

Andreason utilised a list of 102 life events developed by Dohrenwend and her colleagues (1973), each of which was weighted for the amount of stress it caused to the individual who experienced it. A short list of 23 items was used for the purposes of this study which measured six domains related to schooling, job, marital status, household composition, residence and financial status of respondents. Respondents were asked to say whether the impact of any status change, as specified by the list, was positive or negative. In respect of each item therefore, respondents were asked three questions: Did this event occur in your life in the last six months? (If it occurred) Was it a major or minor event? On balance, would you describe its impact as positive or negative?

In addition, respondents were asked to indicate how frequently they had been experiencing six different indicators of stress over the previous six months. Lifestyle was measured in terms of involvement in several activities or decisions to change appearance through their clothing or hair-style in the last six months. Finally, respondents were asked whether they were satisfied with their purchases more often, less often or about the same as ever.

Results indicated that life status change *per se*, regardless of the type of change, can affect consumerism. Life status change can produce stress and this will heighten the individual's effort to adjust his or her lifestyle. Lifestyle change is negatively associated with changes in overall purchase satisfaction. Changes in lifestyle can lead to changes in brand preferences, but at the same time an increased likelihood of dissatisfaction with brands. These findings suggest that consumers under stress, due to changes in their circumstances, may be more open to the suggestions of advertising and brand promotions. This result, if reliable, points to the significance of status change as a market segmentation criterion.

In interpreting Andreason's findings, however, it is important to bear in mind certain limitations to the study. First, the data are based on self-report information from respondents, which can suffer from distortions of memory. Second, the instruments used in this study could have been subject to response bias, such as yea-saying or particular scale-response tendencies. Third, life change was examined cross-sectionally at one point in time rather than longitudinally over time. Thus it is not possible from this piece of research to make statements about temporal cause–effect relationships. Fourth, the database was too small to differentiate among different kinds of life status change. Thus, it is not possible to say if different changes in brand preferences were related to specific life status changes – such as changes of job or in the size of family.

Income and expenditure patterns

Markets are generally considered in terms of people with purchasing power. A common method of segmenting the consumer market is on the basis of income. Fashionable speciality shops stocking designer clothing make most of their sales to high-income shoppers. Other retailers aim their appeal at middle-income groups, while still others focus almost exclusively on low-income shoppers.

In most countries income distribution is shaped like a pyramid, with a small percentage of households having high incomes and the majority of families earning very low incomes. However, in a number of the majority of families in the world today, increasingly more and more people have greater amounts of disposable income.

Household expenditures may be divided into two categories: basic purchases of essential household needs, and other purchases made at the discretion of household members after necessities have been purchased. Total discretionary purchasing power is estimated to have tripled since 1950 (in the USA).

How do expenditure patterns vary with increased income? More than 100 years ago Ernst Engel, a German statistician, published what became known as Engel's Laws – three general statements based upon his studies of the impact of household income changes on consumer spending behaviour. According to Engel, as family income increases:

(1) a smaller percentage of expenditure goes on food;
(2) the percentage spent on housing and household operation and clothing remains constant; and
(3) the percentage spent on other items (such as recreation and education) increases.

Are Engel's Laws still valid? Evidence from the USA suggest that to some extent they are. The first law certainly remains true; a steady decline has been observed in the percentage of total income spent on food, beverages and tobacco, and this occurs from low to high-income families. Although high-income families spend a greater absolute amount on food purchases, their purchases represent a smaller percentage of their total expenditure than is true of low-income families. The second law is still partly correct, since percentage expenditure for housing and household operations remain relatively unchanged in all but the very lowest income group. The percentage spent on clothing, however, increases with increased income. The third law is also true, with the exception of medical and personal care, which appear to decline with increased income.

Engel's Laws provide the marketing manager with useful generalisations about the types of consumer demand that evolve with increased income. They can also be useful for the marketer evaluating a foreign country as a potential target market. Just as a demographic measure can be combined for discussion purposes into smaller groups, socio-economic factors can also be viewed as clusters. Three factors may be distinguished: monetary, home ownership and social class.

The monetary factors

It is no secret that a person's educational background, occupation and income are interrelated. There is a direct relationship between these three variables. Generally, the more education a person has, the greater the likelihood of a better position and increased earnings. However, people have varying propensities to buy and income alone cannot always accurately predict purchase behaviour.

One market segment in particular has gained notoriety during the past few years, the young affluent professional sector. As numerous companies have targeted the dual income baby-boomer generations, such new acronyms as 'Yuppies' (Young Urban Professionals), 'Yaps' (Young Aspiring Professionals) and 'Yummies' (Young Upwardly Mobile Mommies) have become part of the marketer's jargon. However, if one is not careful, this media publicity can back-fire. A large number of companies have focused their efforts on the Yuppies, even though they represent a fairly small proportion of the total market population.

Home ownership factors

Among the variables comprising this group are the issues of home owner versus renter, the type of dwelling that households reside in, and household mobility and stability measures. Home owners are better prospects than renters for a number of products and services. Examples include furniture, major appliances and wall coverings (products), and lawn care, exterminating and insurance (services).

The type of dwelling one lives in can also influence purchase behaviour. The owner of a single-family home has different needs (and many similar ones as well) for goods and services to the owner of a multi-family dwelling, townhouse, etc. Household mobility and stability factors are also interesting marketing statistics. The former measures population turnover (influx and exodus) for an area within a designated time frame. These statistics can provide the marketer with very valuable knowledge. Some of this information can be critical in marketing decision making. Here are some examples:

- A stable community may be difficult to penetrate for a new company in the area. Since the residents tend to be older, they are more likely to be set in their ways.
- In an area with a high turnover ratio, it may be easier for a company to attract new customers, but developing long-term customer relationships will probably be more difficult.
- A neighbourhood with many new home owners may be an excellent segment to target for certain types of businesses.

Social class

Social class is a reflection and compilation of many of the afore-mentioned demographic and socio-economic bases. However, there are further key points to be noted about this variable. Traditionally, the lower–lower to upper–upper social class pyramid was the most common method of categorising individuals by caste, although this method was somewhat simplistic. Today more advanced cluster-based, geodemographic systems are frequently used.

BEHAVIOURAL ATTRIBUTE SEGMENTATION

Behavioural segmentation of markets focuses on the psychological and product orientations of consumers. There are three most common bases for this type of market segmentation:

(1) Product usage
(2) Product benefits
(3) Psychological classification

Each perspective has its own particular advantages and disadvantages as a marketing technique. These perspectives will be dealt with under separate headings.

Product usage

This form of classification examines consumers' product buying patterns. Do they ever buy the product? Do they ever buy the brand? How often do they buy this type of product or this particular brand? If the brand is unobtainable, do they refuse all substitutes (i.e. how brand loyal are they)? Such questions, relating to consumption patterns, are sometimes termed *direct* or *market* classifiers, as opposed to the indirect classifiers such as demography. Market classi-fiers allow direct targeting of marketing activity, including media planning.

A popular method is to divide consumers into non-users, light users, medium users and heavy users of a particular product or service. An additional classification scheme may be to compare the light users versus the heavy users consumption segments, whilst ignoring any non-users in a given market.

The *heavy half* theory popularly attributed to Twedt (1962) draws attention to the fact that in many product fields, 50 per cent of consumers will account for 80 per cent or more of consumption. This is not to say that light users or non-users should be neglected, for they may provide the best prospects for future expansion. Nevertheless, heaviness of buying may well be the most simple, logical and profitable way of targeting market operations.

Product orientation or benefit segmentation

Product orientation segmentation focuses upon such attributes as product usage rates together with the benefits derived from the product. These factors may reveal important bases for pinpointing prospective market targets. In addressing the problem of the proper strategic positioning of a brand, the benefit segmentation approach is a very powerful one. It can be used to identify the key segments in any given market and, once a target segment has been chosen and copy has been developed, it can be used to select a particularly appropriate sample for copy-testing and to track the results of market campaigns aimed at specific benefit segments. This, in turn, gives insights into not only whether the campaign is working as intended, but also about why it is, or is not working.

Some of the most widely used data for behavioural segmentation are provided in the UK by the Target Group Index (TGI) of the British Market Research Bureau Ltd. The index is a national product and media survey which collects information from 24000 adults each year. The service is available on a subscription basis to advertisers, advertising agencies and media owners.

TGI measures, first, heavy to light usage for over 2500 brands in more than 200 fast-moving consumer product fields. Also usage patterns in other fields are covered, including banking, building societies, airlines, cars, holidays, grocery and other retail outlets. Second, it measures media 'audiences' for approximately 150 newspapers and magazines, the weight of TV viewing and half-hourly viewing behaviour for television, the weight of listening to commercial radio, exposure to outdoor media (posters, etc.) and the cinema.

The survey has been operating for over 20 years. By directly linking brand and product usage data to readership, TV viewing and other aspects of media usage, it is of great value in media planning. TGI also produces evidence of the growth/decline of products and brands over the period since its inception. Changes in demographic characteristics of product/brand consumers in this period are also available. The product fields and brands are analysed by: sex, age and class; standard regions and ITV regions; household income; terminal educational age; marital status; years married; number of children; as well as readership habits, TV viewing and other media usage plus other classifications which may be thought appropriate.

The benefit approach to market segmentation enables marketers to identify market segments by causal factors rather than descriptive ones (e.g., demographics). The belief underlying this segmentation strategy is that the benefits which people are seeking in consuming a given product are the basic reasons for the existence of true market segments. Early experience with this approach indicated that benefits sought by consumers determined their behaviour much more accurately than did demographic characteristics or volume of consumption.

This does not mean that the kinds of data gathered in more traditional types of segmentation are not useful. Once people have been classified into segments in accordance with the benefits they are seeking, each segment is contrasted with all the other segments in terms of its demography, its volume of consumption, its brand perceptions, its media habits, its personality and lifestyle, and so forth. In this way, a reasonably deep understanding of the people who make up each segment can be obtained, and by capitalising on this understanding, it is possible to reach them, to talk to them in their own language and to present a product in the most favourable light possible.

The benefit segmentation approach is not a new one. It has been employed by a number of large corporations in the United States, for instance, since it was introduced in February 1961 in an unpublished paper by Haley, titled 'Experimental Research on Attitudes Towards Shampoos'. However, case histories have not frequently featured in published journals because most of the research that has been carried out on this topic has been proprietary. The benefit segmentation approach is based upon being able to measure consumer value systems in detail, together with what the consumer thinks about various brands in the product category of interest. While this concept may seem simple enough, operationally it is very complex. There is no simple, straightforward way of handling the columns of data that have to be generated.

The power of the approach has led to what has been called a generic segmentation study, which is one done mindlessly and mechanically, following specific steps by rote under the assumption that clear-cut and insightful segments will somehow pop magically out of the welter of statistical output generated. Usually this doesn't happen, although once in a while for very lucky people it does. In general, however, the generic segmentation study is likely to be a disappointment to most of the people involved in it. The exception might be the research agency that recommended the generic segmentation study in the first place.

Benefit segmentation (Haley, 1968) is a pragmatic and managerially useful technique that has successfully withstood the test of time (Haley, 1984a, 1984b). While applications of the procedure differ among researchers, a typical approach entails the following steps:

(1) Data are collected on several batteries of variable related to a particular product class. Variables may include product-benefit importance, brand perceptions, product usage and user characteristics.

(2) Some type of clustering technique or combination of factor analysis and clustering is used to partition the respondents into two or more non-overlapping clusters (segments).

(3) Clusters are typically described in terms of averages (i.e., centroids) of the variables used in developing the clusters.

(4) The clusters are then related to still other variables (e.g., demographics) not included in forming the clusters. Multiple-discriminant analysis is often used for this purpose.

(5) The resulting (descriptively embellished) segments are examined for possible strategic implications, relating to new product design, advertising these developments, target market definition, and so on.

Whilst this prototypical approach has been reported as highly useful in many studies, there is no guarantee that the results are stable over time or location (Yuspeh and Fein, 1982; Calantone and Sawyer, 1978). Moreover, large scale segmentation studies are known to be both expensive and time-consuming. Not surprisingly, researchers have often sought simpler approaches with a narrower focus. For example, Haley (1971) has described surveys that mainly centre on the development of advertising themes. Moorthy (1984) has discussed the advantages of consumer self-selection. In this case, products or messages are designed to deliver alternative bundles of benefits that interested consumers will see out. Therefore, it is not necessary to know who selects each benefit bundle but simply the relative size of each segment.

Green, Kreiger and Schaffer (1985) describe a method called BUNDOS (Benefit Bundle Optimization and Segmentation). This represents a market segmentation technique which takes data on sets of benefits of products endorsed by consumers and finds an optimum solution of bundles or segments which maximises the number of respondents whose endorsements are included.

Stability of benefit segments

How stable and reliable are benefit segments? Are benefit segments transient or long-lasting? A major use of identified market segments is as an input to marketing planning about what marketing strategies should be used for various segments. This use leads to the need for control procedures to assess the success of a strategy directed to a particular segment or segments. If a benefit segment identified at one point in time does not change drastically in terms of desired benefits or its size over time, product positioning and advertising appeals targeted at this segment do not have to be changed. If the demographic characteristics of people in each benefit segment also do not vary over time, any media strategies based on unique media habits of target segments can be maintained.

However, if changes in one or more of the initial benefit segments are observed, targeted marketing strategies may have to be changed. If the bundle of benefits desired by a segment changes, then product positioning and advertising appeals will have to be revamped. The benefits sought by a segment might remain similar over time, but the size of that segment might change. If the segment becomes significantly smaller, a strategy initially aimed at this segment might be judged as no longer profitable. Conversely, an increase in segment size may suggest a reallocation away from other (now smaller) segments to the (now) larger segment(s). Finally, the sought benefits and size of an initially identified segment might remain essentially the same over time, but the demographic characteristics of that segment might change. This shift might occur because, although the same people are seeking the same benefit bundle, their demographic features change (i.e., they grow older, more affluent, etc.); alternatively, the type of people who are seeking a given set of benefits might change over time. In either case, such demographic shifts, if they occur, may signal the need for a different kind of media strategy for promotions aimed at the segment.

Calantone and Sawyer (1978) examined the stability of benefit segments over time. Benefit segments based on the relative importance of product attributes were shown to be internally consistent between split halves of a sample for a given period. Two years later, a comparison of the same households segmented in terms of sought benefits revealed a high degree of similarity in product attributes considered important and segment size. However, analysis on an individual household basis showed that a household was very likely to be classified in a segment other than its previous group designation.

In this study Calantone and Sawyer investigated benefit segments relating to the retail banking market. Each respondent's sought benefits were measured by ratings of the importance of 17 attributes associated with banks. Five segments were derived: Front Runners, Loan Seekers, Representative Group, Value Seekers and One-Stop Bankers. Comparisons of segments over time produced similar results. The same five segments emerged following a two-year lag from the first survey. The sizes of the benefit segments each time were similar though not identical. There were also some changes in the demographic characteristics of the segments. At an individual respondent level there was evidence of considerable cluster/segment switching. Only 29 per cent of the consumers remained in the same segment they had been in during the first survey – only marginally greater than chance expectation. These switches were mostly random.

In summary, the results of this study offered confidence that benefit segment solutions were internally consistent within a given time period. Furthermore, a given set of attribute importance was likely to remain relatively intact over time. However, it seems advisable to monitor benefit segments over time because some changes in attribute importance, size and demographic composition are to be expected. Thus, marketing strategies may need to be revised taking into account the ways benefit segments evolve.

Haley (1984a) provides another example of benefit segmentation research. The objective of this study was to identify some of the larger market segments emerging from the many changes in eating habits that seemed to be occurring at the time. The overall research design selected investigated backwards and forwards benefit segmentation techniques.

The 'forwards' aspect refers to the normal approach to benefit segmentation. In general terms this involves a three-step process:

Phase 1: Exploratory research to develop a complete enumeration of benefits of possible value in segmenting the market of interest.

Phase 2: Scale development work to evolve sensitive and reliable measures of major attitude dimensions.

Phase 3: Quantitative measurement of the market. This usually involves a national sample. Respondents are clustered by their attitudes and individual clusters (or segments) are described in terms of their behaviour, lifestyles, demographics and their relevant characteristics.

Under this approach segments are maximally discriminated by their attitudes and differences in behaviour are analysed through cross tabulations.

The backwards approach begins with behaviour. Respondents are clustered on the basis of their behavioural patterns, and the behavioural clusters (or segments) are described by their attitudes, lifestyles, demographics, etc. In other words, segments are maximally discriminated by their behaviour and differences in attitudes are analysed via cross tabulation.

Which is the better approach? Is it better to start with attitudes and look for reflections of those attitudes in behavioural differences and try to explain those by looking for differences in attitudes? Ideally, one would like to have both approaches. If one were forced to make a choice, however, one would like to know first how much reliability one would have to give up to have a valid measure, and vice versa.

Psychological segmentation

Psychological classification of markets has evolved from two principal types of consumer variable: personality profiles and lifestyle profiles (psychographics). Psychological profiles are often used in addition to geographic and demographic segmentation. While the traditional bases of age, sex, education, income, family status and location provide the marketer with accessibility to consumer segments through orthodox communication channels, such as newspapers, radio and television advertising and other promotional outlets, psychological profiles provide important flesh on these geodemographic bones enhancing understanding of the behaviour of present and potential target markets.

Psychographics

While historically the area of psychographics can be traced back to research done in the 1930s, it was extensively developed by marketers and advertisers during the late 1960s, in response to the pressing needs of marketers for better insights into their consumer markets. To appreciate the nature of psychographics, however, we need to think back to the topic of demographic information about consumer markets. Demographics (age, income, sex, etc.) had been available for a long time, and provided useful insights for marketers. During the 1960s, however, marketers began to extend traditional demographic information into the area of consumer lifestyles. This reflected additional reality concerning how products and services could be used to serve activities in daily living.

Pure demographics research could not capture what was going on in consumers' minds – marketers also came to desire information of a psychological nature as well. Until the development of psychographics, two types of psychological information had been available: motivation and personality research. Both these streams of research failed to satisfy marketers' needs. Motivation research had been questioned on grounds of the representativeness of its very small samples and the validity of its meaning, while personality research continued to be plagued with consistently low correlations with consumer behaviour.

Was it possible though to combine the strengths of these approaches into a new consumer research approach? Could new measures be constructed that portrayed consumers' personal fears, needs and desires (as motivation research did), but within large samples that could be quantitatively analysed (as personality research did) and that could also reflect the different types of lives that these people were living (as demographics did)? Several groups of researchers thought that this could be done, and set out to develop psychographics as an area of study.

Psychographics represents one aspect of psychological market segmentation. Psychographics can be distinguished as a marketing technique from the application of personality profiles both conceptually and methodologically. Conceptually, consumers are classified in terms of their values and lifestyles, which are distinct from (though not unrelated to) personality. Methodologically, psychographic instruments tend to be original measures often tailor-made to elaborate and define segments within specific product or service target markets. They are not standardised personality tests originally developed in clinical or academic contexts. At this point, it is perhaps worth saying more about the two concepts of values and lifestyles.

Values

Values are generalised beliefs or expectations about behaviour. Values are important lifestyle determinants and are broader in scope than attitudes or the types of variable contained in AIO (Activities, Interests and Opinions) measures.

Individuals are not born with their values. Rather, values are learned or passed on from generation to generation in society or from member to member in a subcultural group. Many values are relatively permanent from generation to generation but others undergo considerable change. The values most in transition frequently are of most importance to marketing strategists because they provide the basis for difference among lifestyle market segments. They may hold the key to growth for marketing strategists seeking to understand and predict fashions, opportunities or challenges for a purchaser company or industry.

Two types of force may be isolated and analysed in understanding values in a society. The first type of force is the *triad of institutions*: families, religious institutions and schools. The second type of force is *early lifetime experiences*. Government and the media are among the forces that can have an important influence on values. As long as the major institutions are stable, the values transmitted are likely to be relatively stable. When institutions change rapidly, however, the values of consumers also change, causing serious discontinuity in the effectiveness of communication and marketing strategies.

Lifestyles

Lifestyles are the patterns in which people live and spend time and money. Lifestyles are the result of the mix of economic, cultural and social forces that contribute to a person's human qualities. Most directly, lifestyle is a distribution of the social values and personality of an individual.

In practice, lifestyle classification derives from two different perspectives. First, we often come across popular references to lifestyle in the media which provide thumbnail caricatures of certain trendy consumer groups, invented by journalists and qualitative researchers. These lifestyles offer the consumer packaged lifestyle options on which to spend their discretionary income. Hence come Yuppies, Sloanes, Fogeys, Guppies, Dinkies, Swells and their ilk. While these titles may provide readable public relations material, they have limited value for marketing purposes unless based on detailed quantitative research.

Second, there is a more systematically determined concept of lifestyle built upon the social–psychological theory that people develop constructs with which to interpret, predict and control their environment. These constructs or patterns result in behaviour patterns and attitude structures maintained to minimise incompatibilities and inconsistencies in a person's life. Thus it is possible with appropriate quantitative research techniques to measure patterns among groups of people called lifestyles.

Psychographics measures are an operational form of the lifestyles concept. Other factors which can be used to define lifestyles include the cultural transformational triad (family, religion, schools) and early biographical, lifetime experience.

Two basic types of measures are used in lifestyle research. One type – probably the most common – uses general lifestyle items that are intended to determine the overall patterns of living or basic constructs that affect a person's activities and perceptual processes. General statements allow the consumer researcher to define overall patterns such as satisfaction with life, family orientation, price consciousness, self-indulgence, religious beliefs and so forth. Frequently, product specific statements are used which relate to the opinions consumers hold about particular purchases.

CONCLUSION

Four different, but related, complementary rather than opposing, market segmentation strategies have been introduced. The question remains however: What are the hallmarks of successful segmentation studies?

- *clearly defined objectives*, usually focusing on the development of communication strategies rather than on new products.
- *careful organisation*, usually involving the creation of a project team consisting of people from the creative, research and account or brand management areas. Ideally, the team should contain at least a couple of people with previous experience in segmentation research – preferably not all people from the same outside research organisation.
- *a substantial amount of up-front work*, which will involve reviewing past advertising, past research, and significant market factors and trends. As a rule of thumb, about a quarter of the time and project budget ought to go into this area.
- *a three-phase research design*, the second phase of which is the development of sensitive and reliable measures. While it is tempting in the interests of saving time and money to eliminate the second or 'measurement instrument' development phase, to do so will substantially decrease the chances of getting clear results.
- *a thorough examination of alternative modes of segmentation*. There are, as we have already seen, four general types: geographic, demographic and psychographic as well as benefit segmentation. Allow for several possibilities to be built into the research.

- *well-developed plans for follow-through activities.* At a minimum, these should include copy testing in the target segment and tracking studies to obtain feedback on how the various market segments are responding to the marketing action taken.

Few would argue that a sensitive and subtle market segmentation strategy is not a good idea. However, the question remains as to the best available method of segmentation. This book will focus on one of the least understood but potentially most powerful approaches – psychographics.

2 History and background of psychographics

INTRODUCTION

According to some writers (Demby, 1974), the origin of psychographics can be traced back to the work of Paul Lazerfeld and his associates at the Bureau of Applied Research (Lazerfeld, 1935). Lazerfeld suggested that any research aimed at understanding consumer behaviour must 'involve an interplay among three broad sets of variables: predisposition, influences and product attributes'. He did not present a formal model of the interrelationships of these sets of variables, but he did open a door through which many researchers passed en route to a 'humanised' approach to quantitative research.

Among the early landmark papers were those by Lazerfeld (1935) and the Opinion Research Corporation (1959a, 1959b). Other studies are also notable in representing an early psychographic approach (*Harper's Magazine*, 1962) and application of personality research to the marketing context (Dichter, 1958).

During all this development, there was, and even today there still is, disagreement as to what should be included in psychographics and what should not. Describing the development of psychographics, Bernay (1971) wrote that 'Psychographics had its origins in motivation research and in the later attempts by such researchers as Koponen, Gottlieb, Eysenck and many others, to relate personality variables to product choice'. Other researchers sought to separate psychographics from lifestyle research by:

> reserving the term 'psychographics' for measures that are truly 'mental' – attitudes, beliefs, opinions, personality traits, etc. The analysis and classification of activity or behavioural reports from the consumer which are frequently classified as 'psychographics' should be given their own distinct term, such as 'lifestyle'.
>
> (Dorny, 1971: 200)

The historical background of psychological segmentation does not portray a clear, structured path of development, but rather one which has grown on an *ad hoc* basis over a fairly lengthy time period. There are two principal components to the growth of psychological profiling of consumers. The first comprises the application of clinically developed *personality tests* to the consumer context. The second line of development consists of attempts by marketing researchers to produce *original instruments* designed to segment markets in terms of consumers' activities, interests and opinions. Initial developments can be traced back to over 30 years ago.

In the early 1950s advertising and marketing were host to an extensive and lively fad that came to be known as *motivation research*. Armed with 'projective techniques' from clinical psychology and some exciting notions from psychoanalysis, motivation research practitioners attempted to penetrate deeply into the consumer's psyche, revealing for the first time to their astounded clients, the 'real' and often paradoxical reasons why people buy products.

The marketing establishment's reaction was predictable. Conventional marketers insisted that motivation research was unreliable, invalid, insufficiently objective, too expensive, liable to be misleading and that whatever was good about motivation research had long been standard practice anyway. The motivation researchers replied that conventional research was sterile, dull, shallow, rigid and superficial.

Although researchers originally interested in the study of consumer motivation eventually moved on to new and different perspectives, the early 'motivation' research approach left a legacy. It added a human psychological dimension to the usual hard statistics used by marketers to describe and define markets. Subsequently, research which examined consumers' activities, interests and opinions – variously called psychographics or lifestyles research – gained momentum and provided operational techniques for measuring such entities. With these techniques, marketing researchers were able to compose psychological portraits of consumers. These portraits revealed characteristics of consumers which were (highly) relevant to their consumer preferences and behaviours.

Further advantages offered by psychographics research were that it could help advertisers and marketers to 'visualise' their audiences more effectively, and this could, in turn, help them to communicate more effectively to the people they most wanted to reach. Psychographics provided insight into the 'quality' of a target market by drawing a portrait of a product's consumer. Psychographics was also believed to reveal interesting insights into users of particular mass media and hence guide advertisers in the selection of media in which to place their adverts.

One of the early concerns with the psychographics approach to market segmentation was the rather piecemeal fashion in which it had developed. Hustad and Pessemeier (1974) noted the 'atheoretical' foundation of psychographics and argued that this was due to the fact that there was no obvious base to build upon since the area had not been guided by an explicit theory of human behaviour. This stance has, however, been refuted by Reynolds and Martin (1974) who believe that much of the work on lifestyle and psychographics can be seen as 'nested' within Kelly's theory of personal constructs, though this is debatable. Certainly it is true to say that no one psychological theory informs research on psychographics.

Wells (1974) later identified two traditions which eventually amalgamated to be termed variously lifestyle, psychographics, and attitude and opinion research. The first direction has its roots in personality research. Dichter (1958, 1964) produced motivational studies on consumers which stimulated researchers to try and apply concepts of personality and clinical psychology to virtually every aspect of marketing. Koponen (1960) produced the first of many studies incorporating personality inventories. However, in general these studies have produced low correlations, and the relationships which have been uncovered have been too abstract to be useful or actionable by marketing executives. The second direction was that followed by practitioners of motivational research, and this proved to be more successful despite defective methodology. This work sprang from a general realisation that traditional demographic and socio-economic classification and segmentation systems lacked information which could give a greater insight into the consumer.

Wells (1975) pinpointed the mid-1960s as the time when these two directions began to blend to form the psychographic or lifestyle area. Bernay (1971) noted the origin, theory, agreed methodology and current status of psychographics: 'Psychographics had its origins in motivation research and in the later attempts by such researchers as Koponen, Gottlieb, Eysenck and many others, to relate personality variables to product choice'.

CLARIFYING THE DEFINITION OF PSYCHOGRAPHICS

Although two decades have passed since then, many questions about the theoretical history of psychographics remain unanswered. Perhaps the most important is the very definition of psychographics. Some have used the term to refer to basic personality characteristics, e.g., aggression or extroversion; some have applied it to lifestyle variables. Others have preferred definitions involving attitudes, values and beliefs considered more directly pertinent to the product under investigation. Ziff (1971) discussed in some detail various differences in the definition, whilst Wells (1975) revealed the rather startling fact that 24 articles he reviewed on psychographics contained no less than 32 definitions!

Demby (1974) proposed a thorough three-level definition of psychographics. Generally, he stated that psychographics can be seen as the practical application of the behavioural and social sciences to marketing research. On the second, more specific level, psychographics is a quantitative research procedure that is recommended when demographic and other analyses are not sufficient to explain and predict consumer behaviour. On a third, and most specific level, psychographics seeks to describe the human characteristics of consumers that may have a bearing on their response to products, packaging, advertising and public relations efforts. Such variables may span a spectrum from self-concept and lifestyle to attitudes, interests and opinions, as well as perceptions of product attributes.

Much confusion has arisen over the terms lifestyle and psychographics. Lazer presented a definition of lifestyle.

> Lifestyle is a systems concept. It refers to the distinctive or characteristic mode of living, in its aggregate or broadest sense, of a whole society or segment thereof. It is concerned with those unique ingredients or qualities which describe the style of life of some culture or group, and distinguish it from others. It embodies the patterns that develop and emerge from the dynamics of living in a society.
>
> (Lazer, 1963: 131)

Lazer also proposed, in conjunction with this definition, a lifestyle hierarchy (see Figure 2.1).

One similarity between psychographic and lifestyle studies is the relatively straightforward but varied type of the variables employed. Some of the variables are personality traits, like sociability and self-confidence; some are attributes, or interests, or opinions. The descriptions produced are more detailed and more interesting than demographic profiles; and the profiles are more 'psychological'.

There is much overlap between the meanings and usage of the terms of lifestyles and psychographics. Peterson (1972) was one of numerous researchers who have used the term psychographics to

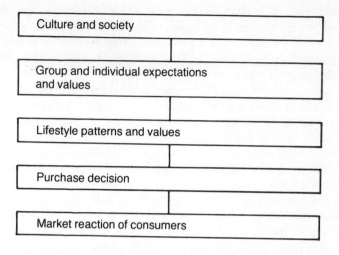

Figure 2.1 Lazar's lifestyle hierarchy

refer to studies that place comparatively heavy emphasis on generalised personality traits (stable, individual differences characteristics like extroversion). Researchers who have preferred the term lifestyle on the other hand, have tended to focus either on broad cultural trends, or more particularly the needs or values thought to be closely associated with consumer behaviour.

QUALITATIVE OR QUANTITATIVE PSYCHOGRAPHICS

Prior to quantitative psychographic research, qualitative research by means of interviews with individuals or groups was the method by which more 'humanised' descriptions of consumers were obtained. One disadvantage of this method was that due to the time and skill consuming nature of the interview technique, the samples were small. They were also unrepresentative as good depth interview respondents were difficult to obtain. A third disadvantage was the tremendous amount of not easily digestible and categorised data that was generated. Often the researcher was forced to rely on some analyst's summary assessment of what was said, so ignoring the very rich and sensitive data that was gathered.

In contrast to this, almost all techniques used in lifestyle and psychographic studies employ objective questions with pre-coded answers. Consequently questionnaires can be self-administered by the average survey interviewer. In addition, data can be transferred immediately and unambiguously from questionnaire to computer. This allows the analyst to make use of both the computer's immense memory and its capacity for multivariable analyses. The growth in lifestyle and psychographic techniques is not coincidentally linked with the computer boom.

A number of different approaches to psychographic analysis have been used over the years. While later chapters will elaborate on each of these applications, a brief overview will be presented here to set the scene. Psychological variables employed in the service of consumer segmentation can be split according to whether they have applied personality traits, operationally developed in clinical diagnosis contexts, to the consumer context or whether they compromise those instruments developed specifically for market segmentation purposes. In either case, further divisions are possible according to the range of application. Thus, some researchers have attempted to produce universal typologies with which to segment all consumers, regardless of any particular buying behaviours they might have. Others have focused on market segmentations in respect of specific product categories or even more narrowly in terms of single product purchase behaviour.

Personality traits

Using this approach, marketing researchers draw upon personality theories and personality tests and measures associated with those theories to classify consumers. This method of consumer segmentation may highlight the fact that the tests and measures being used have been extensively used before and provide tried-and-tested techniques. The problem with this approach is that the personality variables may not travel well from clinical to consumer applications. The use of 'off-the-shelf' tests may be convenient but not always relevant. Personality trait descriptors have been used to provide fairly generalised consumer typologies (Kinnear, Taylor and Sadrudin, 1972) and also in connection with purchase behaviour for particular categories of products (e.g., Koponen, 1960). A detailed discussion of personality traits and consumer classification is presented in chapter 3.

General lifestyle dimensions

Psychological profiles of consumers have been based on general lifestyle dimensions. These studies are not designed around the users of any particular product category or single product. What they have attempted to produce are broad-based population typologies embodying general value systems or clusters, or attitudes and beliefs which distinguish people in general and which can be used as a guide on how people behave in the consumer purchase context. These psychographic profiles can reveal characteristics of consumers which standard demographics do not touch upon, and which have relevance to market movements or marketing campaigns.

These consumer typologies have not always proven to be successful, however, and there have recently been cases of well-known and widely marketed systems of consumer classification being replaced by new ones, due to the lack of effectiveness of the original typologies (see the discussion of VALS in chapter 4).

Product-specified approaches

Many custom-built psychographic measures have tended to focus on users of particular products. These typologies tend to compromise a relatively narrow range of dimensions, but this does not matter because the focus is on being able to make specific statements about consumers' purchase habits in respect of certain products only. These instruments concentrate on the reasons for purchasing specific products and the benefits consumers believe they gain from using them. Such psychographic systems can yield important insights into consumers' perceptions of products because these perceptions are concerned with specific, concrete items with which consumers usually have some familiarity. They can be more relevant to marketing strategies for products than generalised lifestyle inventories.

Combining approaches

The best of both worlds may be obtainable through skilful mixing of the generalised and specific approaches. Broad-based consumer typologies could be integrated with product-specific consumer classifications to provide a broad steer and more focused, and directional indications for specific products.

Wells (1974) describes the procedure by which lifestyle and psychographic data are used to derive new segments from 'direct, object-specific attitude measures' (Hustad and Pessemeier, 1974). After developing a set of lifestyle and psychographic items all related to the topic of the investigation, it is helpful to develop a set of more generalised lifestyle or psychographic items and set of questions about brand or product use, in order to provide additional information but not to be used in constructing the segments. The respondents are clustered on the basis of the responses to the product-specific related items, using cluster analysis or Q-factor analysis to put respondents into a set of exhaustive and mutually exclusive groups. Finally, cluster memberships are cross-tabulated with responses to the items from which the clusters were formed, with the lifestyle and psychographic items not used in the clustering and with the usual demographics. The results of this procedure are often very valuable. Since the segments represent sub-groups with different sets of priorities, marketing executives can create a position, and promote a new brand which reflects the values and properties of a particular sub-group.

Now that the different approaches to psychographic analysis have been outlined, attention must be turned to the question of what are psychographic variables. Demby (1974) describes three classes of psychographic variables. One of these comes under the heading of *product attributes,* a category which incorporates many descriptions of the product, viz. values, perception, taste, texture, quality, benefits and trust. A second category comes under the title of *lifestyle attributes,* which are considered an integral part of psychographic research. There are three main sources from which lifestyle items originate. Brainstorming meetings, and group sessions and depth interviews are two, with the third source being literature in psychology, sociology and anthropology. The final classification of psychographic variables falls under the heading of *psychological attributes.* These variables are particularly important, as the basic purpose of psychographic research is to put flesh and bones on purely demographical data, humanising it. There are essentially two types of psychological variables – how a person sees themself and what kind of an individual a person is.

The lifestyle attributes describe how people go about their daily business, whilst the psychological attributes try to explain why they do. There is a close link between the two. One amplifies the other; one gives texture to the other.

Over the years, the development of interest in psychographics has not been consistent. Periods of considerable enthusiasm for the potential segmentation power and usefulness of the technique have been followed by periods of scepticism when the technique and methodology have been less extensively used. This chapter has sketched the early history of this psychologically-based perspective on market segmentation. The early studies were characterised by attempts to delineate what was specific to a psychographic segmentation approach and how effective it was. Later researchers attempted to make various distinctions in the different approaches to psychological segmentation of consumers. The next chapter will examine this last issue in more detail.

3 Personality profiling of consumers

INTRODUCTION

Personality, or better yet, the inferred hypothetical constructs relating to certain persistent qualities in human behaviour, have fascinated both laymen and scholars for many centuries. The study of the relationship between behaviour and personality has a long and very impressive history dating back to the earliest writings of the Chinese and Egyptians, Hippocrates and some of the great European philosophers.

An individual's personality represents a set of characteristics that can be used to describe consumer segments. Personality is more deep-seated than lifestyle since personality variables reflect consistent, enduring patterns of behaviour. In the context of market segmentation therefore, it can be reasonably assumed that personality variables are related to purchase behaviour. As will be shown, however, the research evidence has revealed only weak or inconsistent relationships between personality and consumer behaviour. The primary reason for this is that marketers have used personality inventories borrowed directly from clinical psychology. Such personality tests have generally been developed to provide operational measurements of behavioural dispositions such as self-deprecation, authoritarianism and neuroticism and standardised upon populations under clinical diagnosis and treatment. In other cases, personality inventories have been developed in academic contexts from student populations, usually in the context of theory development and refinement. In neither of the above cases has there been any attempt to link personality measures with consumer behaviour or to test their efficacy as predictor variables in marketing contexts.

The personality measures used to describe markets generally depend on the personality theory the researcher feels is most relevant. In the fields of marketing and consumer behaviour, the application of personality variables dates from Sigmund Freud and his popularisers in the commercial world – for instance, the motivational researchers in the post-1945 era. There are four major theories or approaches to the study of personality which have had the strongest impact on market segmentation strategies. These are: (1) psychoanalytic theory (with its further development as motivation theory); (2) social–psychological theory; (3) trait-factor theory; and (4) self-concept theory.

The chapter starts by examining the application of the four major personality theories before turning to specific studies of relationships between particular personality variables and consumer behaviour.

PSYCHOANALYTIC THEORY

Psychoanalytic theory posits that the human personality system consists of the id, ego and superego. The id is the source of psychic energy and seeks immediate gratification for biological and instinctual needs. The superego represents societal or personal norms and serves as an ethical constraint on behaviour. The ego mediates the hedonistic demands of the id and the moralistic prohibitions of the superego. The dynamic interaction of these elements results in unconscious motivations that are manifested in observed human behaviour.

The psychoanalytic theories and philosophies of Freud have influenced not only psychology but also literature, social science and medicine, as well as marketing. Freud emphasised the unconscious nature of personality and motivation and said that much, if not all, behaviour is related to the stresses within the personality system. The personality's three sets of forces – id, ego and superego – interact to produce behaviour.

Freud's psychoanalytic theory stresses the unconscious nature of personality as a result of childhood conflicts. The manifestations of these conflicts, particularly the sexual drive, determine the adult personality and frequently influence behaviour in a manner the adult is not aware of. The emphasis on unconscious motives and repressed needs has resulted in a non-empirical approach to the study of personality. Freud's theorists felt that unconscious motives could be determined only by indirect methods. Two techniques were derived from psychoanalytic theory and applied to marketing-depth interviews and projective techniques. Depth interviews were designed to determine deep-seated or repressed motives that could be elicited in structured surveys. Consumers are encouraged to talk freely in an unstructured interview, and their responses are interpreted carefully to reveal motives and potential purchase inhibitions.

Projective techniques were designed to determine motives that are difficult to express or identify, rather than ask consumers direct questions they might not be able to answer, or at least readily provide verbal articulations for. Consumers are given a situation, a cartoon, or a set of words and asked to respond. Consumers are projecting to a less involving situation, thus facilitating expressions of feelings and concerns about products.

In one well-known experiment, Haire used a projective technique in the late 1940s to discover why women were reluctant to purchase instant coffee when it was first introduced. He constructed two shopping lists that were identical, except that one included regular coffee and the other instant coffee. Housewives were then asked to project the type of woman most likely to have developed each shopping list. The housewife who included instant coffee in the list was characterised as lazy and a poor planner. These findings demonstrated that many women had a deep-seated fear of buying products like instant coffee or instant cake mixes, out of a concern that their husbands would feel they were avoiding their traditional role as homemakers. As a result of the study, instant coffee was advertised in a family setting portraying the husband's approval.

The psychoanalytic theory served as the conceptual basis for the motivation research movement that was the precursor to lifestyle studies. According to the philosophy of motivation researchers, consumer behaviour is often the result of unconscious consumer motives. These unconscious motives can be determined only through indirect assessment methods that include a wide assortment of projective and related psychological techniques. The use of this approach in marketing these days is however not common. In the USA, Webster and Von Pechmann (1970) used a replication of the Mason Haire shopping list which yielded results different from those of the original research based on psychoanalysis – instant coffee users were no longer perceived as psychologically different from drip grind users.

Perhaps the richest potential source of marketing ideas derived from psycho-analytic theory is Klein's (1983) work on orality and the oral character. For instance, oral characters are more likely to be both smokers and vegetarians. Oral optimists tend to prefer soft, milky foods and oral pessimists hard, spicy and bitty foods. Certainly being able to categorise people into Freudian types like oral, anal and phallic offers a rich (albeit somewhat unlikely) collection of hypotheses about market segmentation.

MOTIVATION THEORY

The influence of the psychoanalytic theories of personality upon explanations of consumer behaviour has been felt more significantly through the application of motivation typologies to markets (Fennell, 1975). Freudian theory, for instance, provided theoretical direction for motivation research in the 1950s and 1960s. In common with other major theorists in this field, Freud proposed an interpretation of personality in terms of one unifying motivational theme. For Freud it was channelisation of the libido; for Adler it was striving for superiority; for Fromm escape from loneliness; for Sullivan the need for human relationships and for Horney coping with anxiety.

The experimental approach to the study of personality provided insight into the manner in which individual predispositions show themselves in overt consumer behaviour. The importance of this insight can scarcely be overstated. To predict behaviour, one must measure more than just predisposition to respond. It is also important to ascertain whether the particular situation is perceived as one that engages the measured predispositions (Bowers, 1973). Individuals classified as comparable in terms of measured predisposition behave differently in different situations. These differences are a function of the degree to which the situation engages the behavioural disposition. For example, individuals high in need for achievement show achievement-related behaviour in situations they perceive as ego-involving or evaluative, but not in situations they perceive as non-evaluative (Atkinson, 1953).

The immediate implication for marketing research is to focus attention on the consumer's perception of the product-use situation. It matters little that a housewife scores high on need for approval if she does not perceive doing the laundry as a situation that engages her need for approval. This suggests that when only personality disposition is measured, marketing research practice falls short of the mark. The evidence attests to the meagre explanatory power of personality constructs for consumer behaviour (Kassarjian, 1973).

Psychologists who study the effect of personality predisposition on behaviour have attempted to integrate situational factors into their research, and the need for situational sampling raises at once the question of a definition of the population of situations to be sampled. If marketing researchers are to integrate a situational focus into the study of consumer motivation, a classification of motivating situations is called for. The availability of such a classification for use in motivation research will allow the consumer to indicate how he or she perceives the product-use situation in motivational terms.

SOCIAL THEORY

Social–psychological theory differs from psychoanalytic personality theory in two important respects. First, social variables rather than personality determinants are seen as critical in shaping personality. Second, behavioural motivation is directed to meet those ends: i.e. social rather than strictly individual factors.

In his lifetime, several of Freud's inner circle became disillusioned with his insistence on the biological basis of personality and began to develop their own views and their own followers. Alfred Adler, for example, believed that the basic human drive is not the channelisation of the libido but rather the striving for superiority. The basic aim of life, Adler reasoned, is to overcome feelings of inferiority imposed during childhood. Occupations and spouses are selected, homes purchased and cars owned in the effort to perfect the self and feel less inferior to others.

Erich Fromm stressed people's loneliness in society and their seeking of love, companionship and security. The search for satisfying human relationships is of central importance to behaviour and motivation, he claimed. Karen Horney, also one of the neo-Freudian social theorists, reacted against theories of the biological libido, but thought that the childhood insecurities stemming from parent–child relationships create basic anxieties and that the personality is developed as the individual learns to cope with these anxieties.

Although these and other neo-Freudians have influenced the work of motivation researchers, they have had minimal impact on research into consumer behaviour. However, much of their theorising can be seen in advertising today, which exploits the striving for superiority and the need for love, security and escape from loneliness, to sell toothpaste, deodorants, cigarettes and even detergents.

The only recent research in consumer behaviour based directly on a neo-Freudian approach is Cohen's (1968) psychological test examining coping with anxiety – the compliant, aggressive and detached types. Cohen found that compliant types prefer brand names and use more mouthwash and toilet soaps; aggressive types tend to use a razor rather than an electric shaver, use more cologne and aftershave lotion, and buy Old Spice deodorant and Van Heusen shirts; and detached types seem to be the least aware of brands. Cohen, however, admitted to picking and choosing from his data. The Horney typology may have some relevance to marketing intuitively, but reliable demonstration of its predictive accuracy in this context remains to be demonstrated.

Cohen's Compliant–Aggressive–Detached (CAD) test of Horney's classification scheme has been used in marketing research elsewhere (Kernan, 1971). Cohen and Golden (1972) found correlations between CAD, Eysenck's introversion–extroversion variable and Riesman's inner and outer direction variables. Noerager (1979), in a study assessing the reliability and validity of CAD as a marketing measurement instrument, concluded that further development and refinement were necessary.

TRAIT-FACTOR THEORIES

Trait-factor theory represents a quantitative approach to the study of personality. This theory postulates that an individual's personality is composed of definite predispositional attributes called traits. A trait is more specifically defined as any distinguishable, relatively enduring way in which one individual differs from another. Traits can be alternatively considered as individual difference variables.

Three assumptions delineate trait-factor theory. It is assumed that traits are common to many individuals and vary in absolute amount amongst individuals. It is further assumed that these traits are relatively stable and exert fairly universal effects on behaviour regardless of the environmental situation. It follows directly from this assumption that a consistent functioning of personality variables is predictive of a wide variety of behaviour. The final assumption asserts that traits can be inferred from the measurement of behavioural indicators.

The core of these theories is that personality is composed of a set of traits or factors, some general and others specific to particular situations or tests. In constructing a personality instrument, the theorist typically begins with a wide array of behavioural measures, mostly responses to test items, and through statistical techniques distils factors which are then defined as the personality variables.

Trait-factor theory has been the primary basis of marketing personality research. The typical study attempts to find a relationship between a set of personality variables and assorted consumer behaviours such as purchases or media choice (Alpert, 1972). Research also indicates that people can make relatively good judgements about other people's traits and how these relate to their choice of products such as motor cars, occupations and magazines (Green, Wind and Jain, 1972).

SELF-CONCEPT THEORY

Another set of personality measures is based on self-concept theory. This theory holds that individuals have a concept of self based on who they think they are, and a concept of the ideal self based on who they think they would like to be. When measuring these constructs, consumer respondents are asked to describe themselves against each of a list of adjectives, such as dependable, strong, serious, sensitive, aggressive, practical, sociable, confident, and so on. The ideal they would like to attain can be measured in terms of the same attributes by asking consumers to say on which of the items they would like to have as a more or less significant part of their personal make-up.

Self-concept theory has provided two perspectives in its application to marketing problems. First, the discrepancy between self and ideal self is conceived as a measure of dissatisfaction. This measure cannot only reveal the degree of overall discontent with self, but also pinpoint on which attributes this discontent most strongly occurs. This indicator of dissatisfaction could be related to product usage patterns and can be particularly played on in respect of products which purport to offer the consumer a brand of self-improvement.

In one marketing application of self-concept theory, White employed a measure of discrepancy between self and ideal self. He defined three segments based on this discrepancy. High discrepants were dissatisfied with their self-image and wished for great and unrealisable changes; middle discrepants were somewhat dissatisfied and wanted to improve themselves but in a more realistic way; and low discrepants had accurate and often severe notions of themselves, with little tolerance for fantasy. White related these categories to ownership of compact cars, and found that a significant proportion of the middle discrepants owned compact cars. Moreover, they had their current cars for two years longer, on average, than the other two groups. These findings suggested that compact car ownership was greater among consumers with a more realistic, somewhat better adjusted self-perception. The group could be effectively appealed to with a moderate amount of fantasy interspersed with a good dose of reality concerning appeals to durability and economy.

A study by Dolich illustrates self-concept research based on the relationship between self-image and brand image. Dolich studied this relationship for beer, cigarettes, bar soap and toothpaste. He found that respondents tended to prefer brands they rated as similar to themselves on both the actual and ideal dimensions. Several studies have shown the same relationship for cars. An owner's perception of his or her car is consistent to his or her image of others with the same car.

Other research has revealed that the relationship between brand and self-image is somewhat more complicated because consumers change their self-image with the situation. Consumers may, for instance, have different impressions of themselves in social and business contexts. Thus, consumers may buy products to conform with or enhance aspects of their self-image, but that image may change depending on the situation.

There is another dimension of self-concept and its application to marketing. Not only may self-image affect the products consumers choose, but also the products that are chosen frequently as opposed to infrequently. Certain products may have symbolic value, sometimes referred to as 'badge' value. They say something about us and the way we feel about ourselves. Products are thus bought to make a self-enhancing statement.

This extension of self-concept theory has been called symbolic interactionism because it emphasises the interaction between individuals and symbols in their environment. It means that products are bought for their symbolic value in enhancing the consumer's self-concept. It also means that consumers may tend to buy products because of their symbolic associations. The latter, of course, can be conditioned through effective advertising. Self-concept theory as applied to marketing, however, may provide valuable leads as to the kinds of symbolic associations to connect to particular products in order to make them more attractive to their target markets.

One aspect of self, namely self-confidence and an outgoing nature, has been found to be linked to purchase decision-making. Goldsmith (1983) studied the role of venturesomeness in new product purchase by collecting lifestyle items regarding new products from 176 college students using a nominal group technique. The items were combined in a questionnaire with a list of new products combined with a scale to measure self-concepts, person concepts and product concepts. This was given to 73 college students. Correlation of scores on the lifestyle statements with the number of new products purchased confirmed that venturesomeness plays a role in innovative behaviour. The more venturesome subjects viewed themselves as excitable, indulgent, informal, liberal, vain and colourful. However, some early purchasers desired more information before they purchased than did others; these subjects viewed themselves as organisational and rational.

Schaninger and Sciglimpaglia (1981) studied relationships between personality traits and shopping behaviour among 102 housewives in a mid-western American city. In examining shopping information about durable goods on a display board, women with a higher tolerance for ambiguity and higher self-esteem studied the information more thoroughly. Those who were anxious, less confident types drew on less information about goods.

THE APPLICATION OF PERSONALITY VARIABLES TO CONSUMER MARKETS

It is intuitively plausible that personality differences are related to types of product purchased and to the frequency of purchase. More impulsive and extroverted people are more often smokers and drinkers, and engage in a range of more or less anti-social behaviour (Allsop, 1986; Eysenck and Eysenck, 1969). On the assumption of a link between character and consumption some perfumes are given a daring image to appeal to younger, more adventurous women, and car advertisements are variously aimed at sensible, conservative drivers or at sporty, aggressive drivers.

In the 1950s and 1960s a great deal of research was carried out into the relation between general personality traits, such as sociability and emotional stability, and different aspects of consumer behaviour. One classic study (Evans, 1959) attempted, not very successfully, to show personality differences between Ford and Chevrolet owners that matched the distinct brand images of the cars. Koponen (1960) reported that male cigarette smokers scored higher than the average US male in their needs for sex, aggression, achievement and dominance, and scored lower in their needs for compliance and order. Subsequent research has indicated that the relation between personality and cigarette brand choice is highly complex and depends on the sex, social class and self-confidence of the purchaser (Fry, 1971). We will first give an overview of the results from these early studies, summarise the lessons to be learned and then turn to more recent studies of personality.

Reviews of the early literature (e.g., Foxall and Goldsmith, 1988; Kassarjian and Sheffet, 1981; Lastovicka and Joachimsthaler, 1988) are in agreement about the poor quality of much of the research. Perhaps because of this, the findings were very largely equivocal. Some relationships between personality and consumer choice are reported, but these could have been chance findings and generally were not repeated in their studies. At best personality measures only explained 10 per cent of the variation in consumer behaviour, and frequently the figure was less than this.

Of the few positive findings, one concerned Cohen's 'compliant–aggressive–detached' scale, a measure of how individuals cope with anxiety. Men categorised as compliant, aggressive or detached differed in their use of toiletries and in their preferences for brand names. More recent work in psychology has confirmed that people tend to cope with anxiety either by denial or by seeking out more information (repressors versus sensitisers), and awareness of these coping styles could be valuable in designing a marketing strategy for products where anxiety is likely to be prominent.

There are a number of lessons to be learned from the failure of the early studies to produce a greater number of useful findings. Most studies either used unreliable measures or used test batteries such as the Minnesota Multiphasic Personality Inventory and the Edwards Personal Preference Schedule that were never designed to predict specific consumer behaviour. Even more important, little thought was typically given to why a particular measure should be used. Personality traits are relatively stable, and so it makes sense to use them to predict more stable patterns of consumer behaviour rather than one-off decisions to buy brand X and not a largely indistinguishable brand Y (Lastovicka and Joachimsthaler, 1988). Similarly, account must be taken of the conditions under which the variables such as price and convenience would be stronger determinants of choice than personality. Brody and Cunningham (1968) for example, provide evidence that personality is a better predictor of choice of products when consumers perceive the products to differ in significant ways and are confident that at least one product will fulfil their requirements. It is constructive to examine some of these applications of personality scales in more detail.

Dogmatism

Another line of research that proved promising was the relation of the personality trait of dogmatism to consumer innovation. Compared to open-minded, flexible individuals, dogmatic people have been found to be less willing to take risks and to experiment with new products (Jacoby, 1971). Consumer purchasing has also been found to be related to people's self-image – for example, beer drinkers perceive themselves to be more confident, social, impulsive and sophisticated than non-beer drinkers. The importance of self-image is underlined by the fact that people are often willing to describe themselves in terms of products and brands, i.e. 'I'm the sort of person who uses an electric toothbrush'.

A study by Goldsmith and Goldsmith (1980) investigated the possible relationship between dogmatism and confidence in the evaluation of new products. Confidence was thought to be connected with the amount of information needed to make a decision. Following Rokeach's theory concerning dogmatism (Rokeach, 1973), it was suggested that, because they resist new information, highly dogmatic individuals would report that they are more confident than people low in dogmatism in their ability to evaluate a new product. Sixty-two undergraduates were asked to assess their confidence in their ability to evaluate a new product and to complete the Troldahl–Powell Short-Form Dogmatism Scale. The results confirmed the original hypothesis; those students who were rated high in dogmatism reported greater confidence in new product assessment than did those rated low in dogmatism.

Gordon Personality Profile

This instrument attempts to measure ascendancy, responsibility, emotional stability and sociability. Tucker and Painter (1961) examined relationships between these personality characteristics and product use. They used the Gordon Personality Profile and the Sales and Marketing Personality Index which included questions on the use of headache remedies, cigarettes, chewing gum, deodorants, mouthwash and other items commonly purchased by college students. The sample consisted of 133 students. Results showed a relationship between product use and personality traits. This relationship included both frequency of use of particular products and preference amongst different brands of a single product.

Kernan (1971) used decision theory in an empirical test of the relationship between decision behaviour and personality. He added the Gordon Personality Inventory to measure cautiousness, original thinking, personal relations and vigour. Pearsonian and multiple correlations indicated few significant relationships, but canonical correlations between sets of personality variables and decision behaviour have a coefficient of association of 0.77, significant at the 0.01 level.

Sparks and Tucker (1971) found sociability, emotional stability and irresponsibility to be determinant predictors of cigarette smoking, alcohol drinking, shampoo use and early fashion adoption. They also found that a combination of sociability, cautiousness and emotional stability was related to use of headache remedies, mouthwash, late fashion adoption and aftershave lotion.

Edwards Personal Preference Schedule

The EPPS has been used in numerous studies of consumer behaviour. The purpose of the instrument was to develop a factor-analysed, paper-and-pencil, objective instrument to measure the psycho-analytically-oriented needs or themes developed by Henry Murray. Its popularity in consumer behaviour can be traced to Evans' landmark study (1959) in which he could find no differences between 71 Ford and 69 Chevrolet owners to an extent that would allow for prediction. Evans computed a linear multiple regression equation using brand choice as the dependent variable and the ten most discriminating personality variables as independent variables. This equation correctly predicted 88 of the 140 car ownerships (63 per cent) and accounted for 11 per cent of the variance. Using eight demographic variables and the five most discriminating EPPS variables as independent variables, a regression equation correctly identified 89 of the 140 and accounted for 16 per cent of the variance. Evans also submitted samples of the test scores to 18 psychologists with descriptions of Ford and Chevrolet owners derived from motivation research. Collectively, the psychologists guessed car ownership correctly in only 40 per cent of cases. He concluded 'that personality needs, as measured in this study, are of little value in predicting whether an individual owns a Ford or Chevrolet automobile'.

This conclusion has been disputed by several writers who re-analysed his data. For example, Kuehn (1963) was able to raise the predictive accuracy to 90 of 140 by simply subtracting the 'need affiliation' score from the 'need dominance' score. Marcus (1965) was able to correctly predict 91 of 140 by graphically comparing these two need scores. Both the Kuehn and Marcus re-analysis showed that the two EPPS scores correctly identified most Ford owners, but less effectively identified Chevrolet owners. They also showed that the two personality variables were efficient discriminators if the middle range of the distribution was eliminated. These results led other researchers to suggest that there is a need to organise the various influences on the purchase decision, so that conditions can be identified when personality or situational variables are most likely to come significantly into play.

Koponen (1960) found among a sample of 9000 people that cigarette smoking was positively related to sex, dominance, aggression and achievement needs among males and negatively related to order and compliance needs. Further, he found differences between filter and non-filter smokers and found that these differences were made more pronounced by heavy smoking. In addition, there seemed to be a relationship between personality variables and readership of three unnamed magazines.

Using the same data in a study of purchase of coffee, tea and beer, Massy, Frank and Lodahl (1968) concluded that personality accounted for a very small percentage of the variance. In fact, personality plus socio-economic variables accounted for only 5–10 per cent of the variance in purchases.

In another study, Claycamp (1965) presented the EPPS to 174 subjects who held savings accounts in banks or savings and loans associations. His results indicate that personality variables predict better than demographic variables whether an individual is a customer of a bank or a savings and loan association. These results contradict those of Evans who concluded that socio-economic variables are more effective predictors than personality as measured by the same instrument.

In a study of the relationships between personality as measured by the EPPS and consumer decision processes, Brody and Cunningham (1968) argued that the low-level relationships found by previous research could have been caused by inadequate theoretical frameworks rather than providing evidence of the insensitivity of personality measures in predicting consumer behaviour. These writers offered a conceptual model through which to identify the significant sets of factors which affect consumer decision making. This model comprised four kinds of variables:

(1) Personal system variables (e.g., conscious and unconscious needs).
(2) Social system variables (e.g., membership and reference groups).
(3) Exogenous variables (e.g., relative price and purchase convenience).
(4) Risk reducing variables (e.g., trusted retail outlets and brands).

Categorising the multiplicity of variables known to affect consumer behaviour into four groups as such makes them more manageable when analysing their role in a given purchase situation.

Brody and Cunningham (1968) argued that the consumer decision process could be further simplified if the relative influences of each variable system is regarded as a function of the person's perception of the choice situation. They proposed that three perceptions in particular may act as filters to determine the group of variables with the greatest weight:

(1) The perceived performance risk of the decision – to what extent does the person think different brands perform differently in ways that are important;
(2) Specific self-confidence – how certain is the person that the chosen brand will perform as expected;
(3) The perceived social risk – to what extent does the person think that other people judge them by their brand decision.

When combined, therefore, the filtering and classification system indicates where to look for explanatory variables. However, as the authors point out, the model they propose is an oversimplification. Reaction to high perceived risk in respect of a brand is largely dependent on a subjective judgement of risk perceived. Brody and Cunningham explain:

> The effect of performance risks that are matters of personal judgement such as the taste of coffee is probably different from the effect of performance risks subject to objective verification, such as the ability of a toaster to toast bread without electrocuting the user. Refinements, however, can be made after it is shown that the filtering and classification system is a reasonable and fruitful abstraction of reality.
>
> (Brody and Cunningham, 1968: 52)

Brody and Cunningham tested their theory through an examination of the ability of the EPPS to predict brand choice among coffee drinkers. Using a multiple regression analysis they computed relationships between a set of 45 demographic and personality variables and brand loyalty as indicated by claimed frequency of purchase of regular and instant coffee brands. This was done separately among samples of male and female heads of household. Out of this analysis, one male personality variable – need-dominance – and four female personality variables – need analysis, need dependence, need depreciation and consistency – emerged as significant predictors of brand loyalty. Just 3 per cent of the variance was accounted for by the total set of variables, with demographic variables accounting for over half of that.

Next, the same researchers re-analysed their data, but this time within their theoretical framework, which identified those conditions under which personality variables are most likely to be important. More precisely, those circumstances were under conditions of high-perceived performance risk and high specific self-confidence. Under these conditions, these researchers had earlier found that consumers tended to concentrate a high percentage of their purchase on one brand. Guided by this framework, Brody and Cunningham found that as the above conditions became more pronounced in respect of a brand purchase decision, personality variables increasingly explained large amounts of the variance in predicting brand loyalty. In the most extreme case, where consumers concentrated 100 per cent of their purchase on their favourite brand, EPPS variables explained 48 per cent of the variance. Results were even better when comparisons were run across groups showing high degrees of purchase concentration with different brands. Personality variables emerged as powerful discriminators between these high purchase concentration groups.

California Personality Inventory

A widely used measurement technique is a standard psychological inventory, such as the California Personality Inventory (CPI). Robertson and Myers (1969) and Bruce and Witt (1976) developed measures for innovativeness and opinion leadership in the areas of food, clothing and appliances. A multiple stepwise regression with 18 traits on the CPI indicated little variance accounted for; the proportion of variance accounted for was 4 per cent for clothing, 5 per cent for food and 23 per cent for appliances. The study tends to support several previous studies on innovation and opinion leadership that show a minimal relationship between personality variables and behaviour towards new products. Several studies indicate that gregariousness and venturesomeness are relevant to opinion leadership. Two studies have found a relationship between innovation and personality, where three others could find none. Other traits such as informal and formal social participation, cosmopolitanism and perceived risk, are related to innovative behaviour in about half-a-dozen studies, while an additional half-a-dozen studies show no differences.

A study by Boone (1970) attempted to relate the variables on the CPI to the consumer innovator on the topic of a community antenna television system. His results indicate significant differences between innovators and followers on 10 of 18 scales. Vitz and Johnson (1965) using the masculinity scale of both the CPI and MMPI hypothesised that the more masculine a smoker's personality, the more masculine the image of his regular brand of cigarettes. The correlations were low, but statistically significant, and the authors concluded that the results moderately supported product preference as a predictable interaction between the consumer's personality and the product's image.

Consumerism-based personality traits

In an attempt to overcome the shortcomings associated with applying standardised personality instruments, originally developed for clinical purposes, to marketing, some researchers have tried to develop personality measures within a marketing context which therefore have more relevance to the assessment of consumer behaviour.

Worthing, Venkatesan and Smith (1973) questioned earlier studies relating personality traits and product usage patterns because they used tests developed originally for specialised and diagnostic purposes. Worthing *et al.* used scales from Jackson's (1967) Personality Research Form (PRF) which was intended for a wide variety of situations, including consumer behaviour. They found a series of complex relationships between personality traits and product use. The exploratory study indicated that the PRF might overcome the limitations associated with their instruments developed for specialised purposes. However, the results of this replication study did not exactly produce the results of the first study. The PRF offers measures on five factors: affiliation, aggression, dominance, exhibitionism and social recognition. Worthing *et al.* found that affiliation and aggression were related to use of cigarettes, beer, headache remedies, mouthwash and men's dress shorts. Higher personality trait scores were related to greater product usage.

In another study, Fry (1971) not only took advantage of the consumer-based personality measures provided by the Jackson Personality Research Form, but also utilised the conceptual framework of Brody and Cunningham (1968) devised to identify the conditions under which personality variables are most likely to affect consumer behaviour. The focus of attention in this research was upon cigarette brand preferences. In all, ten personality variables were investigated: achievement, affiliation, aggression, autonomy, dominance, femininity, change, sentience, social recognition and self-confidence. The femininity scale was taken from the CPI.

Together with socio-economic variables, personality accounted for between 20 and 30 per cent of the variance in cigarette brand choices. In particular, the study found that a respondent's sex, social class and self-confidence were moderately important predictors of brand selection. Fry concludes that personality variables as measured by standard tests appear to have considerable potential for improving understanding of the psychological basis of brand choice. However, this is only true when research is guided by an appropriate theoretical perspective. It is important to identify which personality traits are important and to define the conditions under which these variables come to the fore.

Reviews of the early literature (e.g., Foxall and Goldsmith, 1988; Kassarjian and Sheffet, 1981; Lastovicka and Joachimsthaler, 1988) are in agreement about the poor quality of much of their research. Perhaps because of this, the findings were very largely equivocal. Some relationships between personality and consumer choice are reported, but these could have been chance findings and generally were not repeated in their studies. At best, personality measures only explained 10 per cent of the variation in consumer behaviour, and frequently the figure was less than this.

Recent applications

More recent research echoes the need to analyse consumer behaviour in more detail. One study investigated the characteristics of female supermarket shoppers as 'Adaptors', who were steady, reliable, efficient and prudent, or as 'Innovators', who were extroverted, open-minded, flexible, assertive and sensation-seeking (Foxall and Goldsmith, 1988). Although purchasers of new brands were more likely to be Innovators than Adaptors, it was the Adaptors that actually purchased the greatest volume of new brands. This was because the Innovators displayed little or no brand loyalty, trying new brands and then quickly abandoning them.

Other research has sought to explore the relationship of open-mindedness to greater consumer choice by using the related personality dimensions of novelty-seeking and sensation-seeking. Hirschmann (1984) distinguishes 'cognition-seeking', the tendency to look for intellectual stimulation, 'sensation-seeking', the tendency to look for a high degree of physical and sensory stimulation, and 'novelty-seeking', the tendency to search out new experiences. Whereas cognition-seeking is more typical of older and better-educated people, who are also more exposed to the mass media, the unrelated trait of sensation-seeking is more typical of younger people who have relatively little mass media exposure and who are not well integrated into society. Novelty-seekers tend to have higher status jobs, be better educated and have more mass media exposure. All three types of experience seeker are more likely to be first-born or only children. This research suggests that it may be helpful to define more carefully the kind of new experience different products offer, and to market them accordingly.

Other personality dimensions are now being investigated that have stronger theoretical links with the processes involved in consumer purchase. The dimension of 'self-monitoring' refers to people's tendency either to adapt to situational or interpersonal demands or to act purely according to their own beliefs and feelings. It has been shown that the more socially-oriented, high self-monitors respond more favourably to advertisements based on selling the image of the product, whereas low self-monitors react better to advertisements stressing a product's quality (Snyder and DeBono, 1985). High self-monitors also appear to be more susceptible to the influence of informal reference groups (Becherer *et al.*, 1979) and they may be more willing to adopt new products (Goldsmith, 1983). A similar construct, inner-directness *vs.* outer-directness, has been shown to be related to car purchase, with the outer-directed (similar to high self-monitors) buying more prestigious cars (McCrohan, 1980).

Internal–external locus of control

This is another personality dimension that is correlated with a wide variety of behaviours. 'Internals' tend to see the events that happen to them as due to their own efforts and abilities, whereas 'Externals' are more likely to attribute events to chance or to the actions of powerful others. People classified as Internals both on measures of general locus of control, and on the more specific health locus of control, go in for more information seeking and preventative health behaviours (Strickland, 1978). This finding is highly relevant to the marketing of health products that are aimed at specific types of consumer rather than people as a whole, or appear to cater for individual needs (Rudnick and Deni, 1980). Examples of slogans appealing to Internals are 'specially developed for sensitive skins' or 'goes only where your hair needs it'.

Religion and religiosity

Some researchers have hypothesised that religious values may be significant constructs in assessing and explaining certain aspects of consumer behaviour. Religiosity has frequently provided a value system around which groups and nations have coalesced. As a fundamental value system, it is reasonable to assume that religiosity may have a role to play in the context of consumer activity.

Studies that have examined the relationship between perceived risk and purchase behaviour have found a direct relationship between the level of perceived risk and brand/store loyalty and the amount of information sought about brands, and an inverse relationship between the level of perceived risk and consumer product trial and innovative behaviour (Jacoby, 1971; Schiffman and Kanuk, 1980). Furthermore, the concept of perceived risk has been treated as a personality construct. The selection of self-confidence as a personality trait is largely consistent with the consumer risk-taking tradition (Hugstad, Taylor and Bruce, 1987).

Varying levels of self-confidence and anxiety can be explained in large part by differences in religious background (Baker and Gorsuch, 1982; Guthrie, 1980; Sturgeon and Hamley, 1979). Non-religious people appear to exhibit greater self-indulgence, less anxiety and the ability to integrate anxiety into everyday life in an adaptive manner (Baker and Gorsuch, 1982; Kahoe, 1984). They also tend to be more flexible, self-reliant, sceptical, pragmatic, and to be less sentimental (Hamby, 1973; Kahoe, 1984).

A recent study which explored the influence of religion and religiosity on perceived risk in purchase decisions compared the behaviour of Catholic and Jewish households in a north-eastern area of the United States (Delener, 1990). Data were collected from those households who had purchased a new car and/or microwave oven within the previous year. Each participant householder supplied information about their perceived strength of religious affiliation and filled in a scale of religious orientation and involvement. For measuring the level of perceived risk, respondents were asked to state performance risk on a nine-point scale in which one represented the lowest perceived risk and nine was the highest, and did so in respect of the purchase of a new car and microwave oven.

The findings indicated that religion and religious orientation may be significant variables in predicting perceived risk in consumer purchase decisions. Religious individuals tended to perceive higher risks in their purchase decisions. This attitude, explained Delener, was related to the tendency of highly religious individuals to be less secure and self-confident than less religious individuals. The findings of this study further suggested that religion and religious orientation should perhaps be viewed as variables having greater potential influence on marketing and consumption. According to Delener, marketing strategists who want to understand consumers in a more predictive and comprehensive manner may find it useful to view religion and religious orientation as generators of consumption patterns rather than simply as correlates of item purchasing.

Cognitive style

As an alternative to segmentation of consumers based upon attitudinal responses which tend to be tied to specific objects or situations, some writers have suggested using the variable termed cognitive style. Cognitive style attempts to describe the manner in which an individual searches for meaning. It is defined as three multivariate sets of influence on cognitive activity – propensity to use certain senses and symbolic forms, orientation to different cultural roles and propensity to reason in different ways.

It has been argued that if cognitive style is related to consumer choice behaviour, then it should offer two distinct advantages over attitude typing. First, cognitive style is not presumed to be situation-specific; once defined it can be applied across all products and brands. Second, cognitive style defines an individual's preferred strategy for seeking meaning, indicating a much more direct and predictable influence on certain behaviour than that of non-strategic attitudes (Furse and Greenberg, 1975). While the attitude construct is undoubtedly much richer in describing the whole milieu of feelings, beliefs and behaviour relating to specific products, cognitive style is presumed to offer a better predictor of information-seeking behaviour in the market-place.

Furse and Greenberg produced a two-fold segmentation in examining men's attitudes towards toiletries. The two segments were labelled 'Mr Practical' and 'The Fun-Loving Routine-User'. Two lesser types were isolated – a type concerned with aftershaves as an adjunct to sexual role-playing and a conservative non-user type – but both categorised considerably fewer respondents than the first two.

Mr Practical was found to be oriented towards practicality. Although a user of aftershave, this type of user generally rejected packaging and advertising influences on brand choice. He disdained promotional images, but agreed with physical sensations, such as cleanliness and freshness, associated with such products. In addition to being pragmatic, 'Mr Practical' was also conformist in his opinions about purchase and use of the product as demonstrated by agreement with statements such as 'women introduce men to colognes by buying them as gifts' and 'men tend to use the same brands as someone else whose opinion they respect'.

The Fun-Loving Routine-User did not consider the use of aftershave and cologne as serious behaviour, but merely a bit of good fun. This segment favoured the use of aftershaves because they were seen as things that are personally pleasant and because they make a person smell better and, perhaps, more pleasant to be around in social situations. This type of person rejected ideas associated with psychological reasons for use of the product, such as 'shaving gives a man self-awareness' and 'aftershave is a sign of masculinity'. However, this person enjoyed the consumption of promotional and advertising images which did not take themselves too seriously. 'The Fun-Loving Routine-User' did not view aftershave as something that is strongly related to sexual behaviour, but did agree that men like to feel attractive to women and cologne reinforces this feeling. In general this type tended to be a routine user of this product and was likely to try a variety of brands.

Attitude was found to be related to response to advertising, specifically for toiletry advertising, but they were not related either to product usage or brand loyalty among this sample. Furse and Greenberg suggest, however, that this result might be due in part to artificial features of the study which used a sample entirely composed of college students and the fact that only two major attitudinal segments were employed as discriminating variables.

The same study also investigated the feasibility of using cognitive style as a market segmentation variable. Cognitive style represents a set of predispositions influencing an individual's information gathering and processing behaviour. Taken together these cognitive style characteristics are presumed to represent relatively stable strategies which regulate how an individual processes his or her everyday experiences. Furse and Greenberg found that their sample was characterised by such cognitive style attributes as an orientation towards processing information through the written word, or through the spoken word or via pictures. Some respondents had relatively strong orientations towards smell, touch and other kinds of sensory input. Cognitive style tended not to be strongly related to product usage or brand preference, but was linked to mass media consumption. For example, respondents with orientations towards the written word exhibited strong preferences for print media, particularly for magazines, while those with an orientation towards the spoken word preferred television. Cognitive style was seen as having potential to guide decision making in the sphere of new product promotion. Knowing about consumers' preferred strategies for processing information could not only help decide upon media placement of promotions but also in respect of the design of the promotional messages themselves.

CONCLUSIONS FROM PERSONALITY RESEARCH

Limitations in comparing early studies in which personality test measures have been related to product usage derive from the variety of instruments utilised, variations in product category definitions, usage rate classifications and brand selections. Even a cursory comparison of selected product categories (e.g., automobile or cigarettes) that have been found to be associated with personality traits (e.g., sociability, emotional stability, ascendancy and the like) reveals inconsistencies. Major shortcomings with studies relating personality test scores and product usage rates have been identified. First, the use of personality instruments on a specific population in a consumer behaviour context is inappropriate in as much as these instruments were originally developed for specialised purposes far removed from situations involving consumer behaviour (Brody and Cunningham, 1968; Kassarjian, 1971; Wells, 1966). Second, Sparks and Tucker (1971) point to an analytical weakness in previous studies. The usage of bivariate, inferential techniques and regression including multiple correlation implies that personality is comprised of a packet of discrete, independent traits which do not interact or exert interrelated influences on one's product brand preferences.

In spite of the lean harvest from early research on personality and consumer behaviour, more recent studies, with measures that are better empirically and theoretically grounded, offer more promise for the future. Among the measures one can tentatively identify at this point as likely to be useful in market segmentation are internal–external locus of control, self-monitoring or inner/outer directness, cognition seeking, sensation seeking and repression–sensitisation. In most cases reliable and valid measures already exist with which to measure these constructs. It will be necessary, however, to specify quite precisely what aspects of consumer behaviour are involved. For example, different personality characteristics may be related to shop and supermarket use, information seeking and appraisal of new products, exposure to different media, willingness to innovate and brand loyalty. Again, stable patterns of consumer behaviour, and behaviours about which consumers feel more subjectively certain, are likely to be more strongly related to personality than are one-off or essentially random choices. A greater appreciation of these factors, and about the salient aspects of personality, should lead to much more effective segmentation strategies in the future.

4 Psychographic systems for consumer profiling

INTRODUCTION

This chapter focuses on the nature and technique of customised psychological profiling of consumer markets. The earliest attempts to segment and classify consumers according to psychological criteria derived from the marketing industry's interests in how consumer behaviour was motivated. This led to the application of classical psychological techniques and theories to measure and explain human behaviour in the context of consumerism. The central question recurs: do techniques and instruments often developed within clinical psychology generalise to this quite different area of human experience and activity?

As earlier chapters have shown, for three decades following the Second World War, marketing researchers tested the efficacy of clinical measures of personality to segment consumers and product buying behaviour with mixed results. Other researchers, believing that more clinically-developed personality tests were not relevant to the marketing context, began to develop their own 'psychological' instruments, whose contents were designed to relate to particular areas of consumer behaviour in a more direct way.

It is important to distinguish these two perspectives and their relative advantages and disadvantages as predictors of consumer behaviour. To begin, we need to be clear about the central concepts and terms, and what they mean. Personality can provide an explanation for why two individuals receiving the same social influences have different lifestyles. Personality measurement may provide an important mediating variable which accounts for individual differences alongside broader categories of economic and social influence that are typically included in lifestyle studies.

The previous chapter reviewed research in which attempts were made to use clinically-developed, standardised personality tests to segment consumer markets. This research effort was not consistently fruitful. Some recent advances in personality research by Horton (1979) indicate that personality variables, such as anxiety and self-confidence, are in themselves related to consumer choice behaviour, but even in this encouraging research for the concept of personality, explanation is stronger in some specific stimulus settings than others, primarily low-risk products.

As we have seen already, a number of studies investigated the hypothesis that personality could be directly related to product choice. A few of these reported some relation between product use and personality traits (Evans, 1959). Most found small amounts of variance in product choice explained by personality (Westfall, 1962; Evans, 1959; Koponen, 1960). It is not surprising that these studies found little relationship between personality and overall brand or product choice. Personality is but one variable in the process of consumer decision making. If any relationship were to be established, dependent and confounding variables such as intention and income would be better candidates than would behaviour.

Even if personality traits were found to be valid predictors of intentions or behaviour, would they be useful as a means of market segmentation? A positive answer would require that the following circumstances prevail:

(1) People with common personality dimensions must be homo-geneous in terms of demographic factors such as age, income or location so that they can be reached economically through the mass media. This is necessary because data are available on media audiences mostly in terms of demographic characteristics. If they show no identifiable common characteristics of this type, there is no practical means of reaching them as a unique market segment.

(2) Measures that isolate personality variables must be demonstrated to have adequate reliability and validity. The difficulties in this respect have been extensive.

(3) Personality differences must reflect clear-cut variations in buyer activity and preferences, which, in turn, can be capitalised upon meaningfully through modifications in the marketing mix. In other words, people can show different personality profiles yet still prefer essentially the same product attributes.

(4) Market groups isolated by personality measures must be of a sufficient size to be reached economically. Knowledge that each person varies on a personality scale is interesting but impractical

for a marketing firm, which, of necessity, must generally work with relatively large segments.

The evidence to date falls short of these criteria, and personality traits have not been convincingly demonstrated as a useful means of market segmentation. There is no reason to assume, for example, that individuals with a given personality profile are homogeneous in other respects; nor does it seem reasonable to expect that they have enough in common to be taught easily through the mass media without attracting a large number of non-prospects.

Research on personality has failed to generate very good prospects. This has stimulated the development of broader, more behavioural concepts that are likely to be better targets for market segmentation – namely lifestyles.

PSYCHOGRAPHICS

Psychographics is the principal technique used by consumer researchers as an operational definition or measure of lifestyle. One aim of psychographics is to provide quantitative measures of consumer lifestyles, in contrast to soft or qualitative research from focused group interviews, depth interviews and similar techniques.

In reaction to the small samples of most qualitative research, consumer analysis previously tried to explain consumers' life patterns in terms of demographics – income, education, place of residence and so forth. While demographics are very important in explaining consumer behaviour, because they define and constrain the life patterns that are possible for most people, they do not go far enough. The concept and name of psychographics were originated by Demby (1974) to describe a technique that added the richness of the social and behaviourial sciences to demographics. Demby provided a three-level definition of psychographics.

(1) Generally, psychographics may be viewed as the practical application of the behavioural and social sciences to marketing research.
(2) More specifically, psychographics is a quantitative research procedure that is indicated when demographic, socio-economic and user/non-user analyses are not sufficient to explain and predict consumer behaviour.
(3) Most specifically, psychographics seeks to describe the human characteristics of consumers that may have bearing on their response to products, packaging, advertising and public relations

efforts. Such variables may span a spectrum from self-concept and lifestyle to attitudes, interests and opinions, as well as perceptions of product attributes.

There has been some dispute between marketing practitioners and academic researchers as to what constitutes psychographics – and whether or not it is synonymous with lifestyle research. The consensus appears to be that there is a distinction between the two concepts. Psychographics refers to a consumer's personality traits (e.g., their sociability, self-reliance, assertiveness), while lifestyles consist primarily of an individual's activities, interests and opinions, or AIOs. In practice, personality traits and lifestyles need to be considered collectively to provide meaningful marketing information.

AIO, a term used interchangeably with psychographics, refers to the measures of activities, interests and opinions. Some researchers use the 'A' to stand for attitudes, but activities are a better measure of lifestyles because they measure what people do. AIO components are defined by Reynolds and Darden (1974) as follows:

An activity is a manifest action such as viewing a medium, shopping in a store, or telling a neighbour about a new service. Although these acts are usually observable, the reasons for the actions are seldom subject to direct measurement. An interest in some object, event or topic is the degree of excitement that accompanies both special and continuing attention of it. An opinion is a verbal or written 'answer', that a person gives in response to a stimulus situation in which some 'question' is raised. It is used to describe interpretations, expectations and evaluations – such as beliefs about the intentions of other people, anticipations concerning future events, and appraisals of the rewarding or punishing consequences of alternative courses of action.

Examples of each AIO category are shown in Table 4.1. Demographics are also undivided in most studies involving such variables.

AIO statements

AIO statements in psychographic studies may be general or specific. In either type, consumers are usually presented with Likert scales in which people are asked whether they strongly agree, agree, are neutral, disagree or strongly disagree. Statements can be administered in person, by phone or by mail, often in mail panels. AIO inventories are developed by first formulating a large number of questions

Table 4.1   AIO categories of lifestyle studies

Activities	Interests	Opinions	Demographics
Work	Family	Themselves	Age
Hobbies	Home	Social issues	Education
Social events	Job	Politics	Income
Vacation	Community	Business	Occupation
Entertainment	Recreation	Economics	Family size
Club membership	Fashion	Education	Dwelling
Community	Food	Products	Geography
Shopping	Media	Future	City size
Sports	Achievements	Culture	Stage in lifestyle

Note: In this approach, respondents are presented with long questionnaires –
sometimes as long as 25 pages. The table above shows the major dimensions used to
measure the AIO elements.
Source: Joseph T. Plummer 'The concept and application of lifestyle segmentation',
Journal of Marketing, 38 (January 1974), 34. Reprinted from the Journal of Marketing
published by the American Marketing Association. Reproduced by permission of the
publisher.

regarding consumer AIOs and then selecting a smaller number of
questions that best define consumer segments.

AIO statements are usually analysed by cross-tabulating each
statement on the basis of variables believed important for market
segmentation strategies, such as gender, age and so forth. Factor
analysis or other multivariate techniques may be used to group the
statements into a more parsimonious format. Factor analysis is a
mathematical technique for examining the inter-correlation between
statements in an attempt to determine common or underlying factors
that explain observed variations.

Specific AIOs

The specific approach to AIOs focuses on statements that are product
specific and that identify benefits associated with the product or
brand. One study concerned with health care services included both
general and specific statements (Blackwell and Talarzyk, 1977). The
study was concerned with predicting what types of consumers try to
behave in a way that will achieve consistency between their behaviour
and attitudes, and it was necessary to determine specific attitudes
toward physicians as well as towards malpractice. Thus, statements
such as the following were included:

(1) I have a great deal of confidence in my own doctor.
(2) About half of the physicians are not really competent to practice medicine.
(3) Most physicians are overpaid.
(4) In most malpractice suits, the physician is not really to blame.

In this study, respondents who indicated that they had a great deal of confidence in their doctors also reported a much lower likelihood of bringing a malpractice suit. Respondents agreeing with statements that physicians are not really competent and that they are overpaid, and disagreeing with the statement that physicians are not really to blame in malpractice suits were more likely not to file a malpractice suit. Respondents who agreed with general AIO statements such as 'I generally do exercises' and 'I am sick a lot more than my friends are' were found also to be more likely to bring malpractice suits. Such findings demonstrate how both general and specific AIOs can be used to profile consumers and relate their lifestyles to behaviour.

Some AIO studies attempt to generate a broader base of lifestyle types which may be applied to more than one product market. For example, Wells and Tigert (1971) formulated 300 AIO statements and asked respondents to agree or disagree with each on a six-point scale. Factor analysis was then used to reduce these 300 statements to 22 lifestyle dimensions. A selection of the results are shown in Table 4.2.

In another study whose purpose was to explore relationships between consumers' lifestyle and their overall product assortment decisions, Cosmas (1982) used a postal questionnaire containing 250 AIO items and 179 frequency-of-use items. A technique called Q-factor analysis was used to compute lifestyle and product topologies. The lifestyle clusters generated were: (1) Traditionalists, (2) Frustrated, (3) Life-expansionists, (4) Mobiles, (5) Sophisticates, (6) Actives and (7) Immediate Gratifiers. The product clusters were: (1) Personal Care, (2) Shelf-stocker, (3) Cooking and Baking, (4) Self-indulgent, (5) Social, (6) Children's and (7) Personal Appearance.

In addition to the above tests, an 'eyeballing' of the data suggested the following relationships. The *Traditionalists'* product assortment decisions were characterised by Shelf-stocking and Cooking and Baking tendencies. This, in turn, seemed to reflect the Traditionalists' way of life, which placed emphasis on the role of women as home-makers. The *Frustrateds'* product assortment decision tended to be weak on the Social dimension and unrelated to any of the others. This indicated that Frustrateds tended to be unsure about what they liked and an inability to find satisfaction in product purchase in any clearly

Table 4.2 Sample lifestyle categories based on perceived activities, interests and opinions

Price Conscious

I shop a lot for specials.

I find myself checking the prices in the grocery store even for small items.

I usually watch the advertisements for announcements of sales.

A person can save a lot of money by shopping around for bargains.

Fashion Conscious

I usually have one or more outfits that are of the very latest style.

When I must choose between the two I usually dress for fashion, not for comfort.

An important part of my life and activities is dressing smartly.

I often try the latest hairdo styles when they change.

Homebody

I would rather spend a quiet evening at home than go out to a party.

I like parties where there is lots of music and talk. (Reverse scored.)

I would rather go to a sporting event than a dance.

I am a homebody.

Child Oriented

When my children are all in bed I drop almost everything else in order to see to their comfort.

My children are the most important things in my life.

I try to arrange to be home for my children's convenience.

I take a lot of time and effort to teach my children good habits.

Compulsive Housekeeper

I don't like to see children's toys lying about.

I usually keep my house very neat and clean.

I am uncomfortable when my house is not completely clean.

Our days seem to follow a definite routine such as eating meals at a regular time, etc.

Self Confident

I think I have more self-confidence than most people.

I am more independent than most people.

I think I have a lot of personal ability.

I like to be considered a leader.

Dislikes Housekeeping

I must admit I really don't like household chores.

I find cleaning my house an unpleasant task.

I enjoy most forms of housework. (Reverse scored.)

My idea of housekeeping is 'once over lightly'.

Sewer

I like to sew and frequently do.

I often make my own or my children's clothes.

You can save a lot of money by making your own clothes.

I would like to know how to sew like an expert.

Canned Food User

I depend on canned food for at least one meal a day.

I couldn't get along without canned foods.

Things just don't taste right if they come out of a can. (Reverse scored.)

Dieter

During the warm weather I drink low

Community Minded

I am an active member of more than one service organisation.

I do volunteer work for a hospital or service organisation on a fairly regular basis.

I like to work on community projects.

I have personally worked in a political campaign or for a candidate or an issue.

Self Designated Opinion Leader

My friends or neighbours often come to me for advice.

I sometimes influence what my friends buy.

People come to me more often than I go to them for information about brands.

Information Seeker

I often seek out the advice of my friends regarding which brand to buy.

I spend a lot of time talking with my friends about products and brands.

calorie soft drinks several times a week.

I buy more low calorie foods than the average housewife.

I have used Metrecal or other diet foods at least one meal a day.

Financial Optimist

I will probably have more money to spend next year than I have now.

Five years from now the family income will probably be a lot higher than it is now.

Source: Adapted from William D. Wells and Douglas I. Tigert, 'Activities, Interests and Opinions,' *Journal of Advertising Research* 11 (August 1971):35. Reprinted from the *Journal of Advertising Research* © 1971 by the Advertising Research Foundation. Reproduced by permission of the publisher.

defined way. The *Life-Expansionists'* product assortment tendencies were characterised by weak dispositions towards Shelf-stocking, Self-indulgence and Personal Appearance. This reflected the Life-Expansionists' way of life which had placed emphasis on involvement with their environment and a rejection of self-centredness. The *Mobiles'* product-related behaviours were characterised by strong Self-indulgent, Children's and Personal Appearance tendencies. The Mobiles' way of life placed emphasis on careful eating habits and more emphasis on themselves and other members of the family due to a lack of social ties. The *Actives'* product-related attributes were characterised by Personal Care, Self-indulgence and Personal Appearance factors. This reflected the Actives' way of life which placed emphasis on meeting people, going places and just 'being on the go'. The *Sophisticates'* product-related characteristics were defined by Personal Care and Social product dimensions. Sophisticates tended to place emphasis on the social and external events in their environment. Finally, the *Immediate Gratifiers* were characterised by Personal Care, Cooking and Baking, Self-indulgence and Social factors. The Immediate Gratifiers desire instant satisfaction and crave hedonistic activities.

LIFESTYLE CONCEPTS AND MEASUREMENTS

Lifestyle as a construct goes beyond that of personality. For marketing purposes lifestyle is more contemporary, sociological, comprehensive and more useful. For these reasons, considerable attention has been devoted to understanding the construct, how it is measured and how it is used. Lifestyles are defined as patterns in which people live and spend their time and money. They are primarily functions of consumers' values.

Consumers develop a set of constructs (ideas, descriptors) that minimise incompatibilities or inconsistencies in their values and life-styles. People use constructs such as lifestyles to construe the events happening around them and to interpret, conceptualise and predict events. Kelly (1955) noted that such a construct system is not only personal, but also continually changing in response to a person's need to conceptualise cues from the changing environment to be consistent with one's values and personality (Reynolds and Darden, 1972a). Values are enduring but lifestyles change much more rapidly, causing researchers to place attention on currency and flexibility in research methods and marketing strategies.

The concept of lifestyle is built upon the social–psychological theory that people develop constructs with which to interpret, predict and control their environment. These constructs result in behaviour patterns and attitude structures maintained to minimise incompatibilities and inconsistencies in a person's life – thus, it is possible to measure patterns among groups of people, called lifestyles. Psychographics or AIO measures, which may be general or product specific, are the operational form of lifestyle, which marketing researchers measure.

The fundamental forces creating lifestyles include the *cultural transfusive triad* and *early lifetime experiences.* The former refers to the influence of institutional influences such as the family, religion and school, while the latter refers to basic intergenerational influences such as depressions, wars and other major events.

There have been several attempts to produce psychological typologies of lifestyle which can cover the entire active consumer population. These studies have generated psychographic segmentations which comprise basic categories of consumers defined in terms of their reported values and lifestyles. These systems are purported to yield enduring psychological constructs which define the broadest consumer populations, but which also predict idiosyncratic behaviour.

One of the most widely popularised approaches to lifestyle research for market segmentation on this scale is the Values and Lifestyles (VALS) programme developed by Mitchell (1983) at SRI, a management consulting firm in California. It started from the theoretical base of Maslow's (1954) need hierarchy and the concept of social character (Riesman, Glazer and Denney, 1950). The essence of the VALS programme is a classification scheme that assigns people to one of nine VALS segments. These segments are determined by both the values and lifestyles of the people in them ('values' within this system refers to a wide array of an individual's beliefs, hopes, desires, aspirations, prejudices and so on). Conceptually, VALS represents a linkage between the personality orientation of psychographics and the activities orientation of lifestyle research.

The 'nine American lifestyles' defined in this programme, together with typical demographics and buying patterns, are shown in Figure 4.1. Another approach called Monitor is available from Yankelovich, Skelly and White, although the SRI or VALS approach appears to be used more often by marketers (Atlas, 1984; Holman, 1984; Yuspeh, 1984). We will examine this system more closely.

Figure 4.1 The original VALS typology

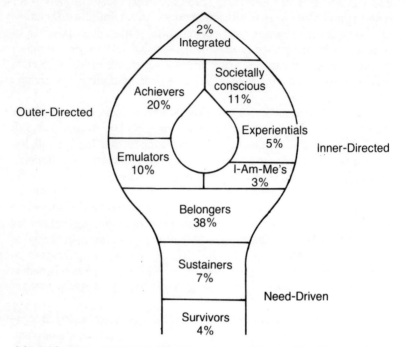

Adapted from: Arnold Mitchell. *The Nine American Lifestyles: Who We Are and Where We Are Going*. New York: Macmillan, 1983 and the Values and Lifestyles (VALS) Program, SRI International, Menlo Park, California.

THE BASIC VALS SYSTEM

The basic belief behind VALS is that humans strive to improve themselves during their lifetime. This goal, in turn, strongly influences their values, lifestyles and many of the decisions they make each day. The approach is holistic, drawing on insights from a number of perspectives and many types of data to develop a comprehensive framework of characterising the ways of life of American people.

The core of the VALS programme is the VALS typology. This typology is hierarchical. The VALS system defines a typology of four basic categories of consumer values and lifestyles, with nine more detailed types. Drawing originally from Maslow, SRI describes consumer market segments as *Need-Driven, Outer-Directed, Inner-Directed* and *Integrated*.

The argument is that there are basic needs which have to be satis-

Table 4.3 Key demographics of the VALS segments

		Age[a] *(median)*	*Sex (% female)*	*Race (% white)*	*Education*[a] *(years)*	*Income*[a] *(household)*
I.	*Need Driven*					
	Survivors	66	60	55	8.5	5000
	Sustainers	32	52	57	10.0	9000
II.	*Outer-Directed*					
	Belongers	54	60	92	11.0	14000
	Emulators	28	48	76	12.5	19000
	Achievers	42	39	95	13.5	35000
III.	*Inner-Directed*					
	I-Am-Me's	20	42	87	11.5	12500
	Experientials	26	61	96	14.0	26000
	Societally conscious	38	54	89	15.0	30000
IV.	*Integrateds*	40	54	93	16.0	34000

Note: [a]Age is expressed as median years, education as mean years completed and income as median 1980 dollars per household in each segment.
Source: SRI International, VALS – *Values and Lifestyles of Americans*, Menlo Park, Calif.: SRI International, undated, p.4. Reproduced by permission of the publisher.

fied to survive and sustain existence. Need-Driven motives give way to expression of the sort of person you are, a development which often accompanies increased affluence, following either the pathways of Outer-Directedness or Inner-Directedness to influence ways of living, products bought and so on.

The prime developmental thrust is from Need-Driven through Outer-Directed and Inner-Directed phases, to a journey of Outer- and Inner-Directions. These major transitions are seen as crucial stageposts in the movement of an individual (or a society) from immaturity to full maturity. By maturity is meant psychological maturity. Very generally, psychological maturation is marked by a progression from partial towards full realisation of one's potential. It involves a steady widening of perspectives and concerns and a steady deepening of the inner influence points consulted in making important decisions.

The VALS topology is divided into four major categories, within each of which there are several segments (excepting the Integrateds which is so small that it is a segment in itself). These lifestyle segments are fitted together into what is called the VALS double hierarchy. In total, there are nine VALS segments, with every adult theoretically fitting into one of these categories. Table 4.3 summarises some of the demographic characteristics of these segments.

The lifestyle groups in the United States include Survivors (4 per cent), Sustainers (7 per cent), Belongers (35 per cent), Emulators (9 per cent), Achievers (22 per cent), I-am-me's (5 per cent), Experimental (7 per cent), Societally-conscious (9 per cent) and Integrated (2 per cent). A proprietary system of weighting questions for classification was developed using data from a national probability sample of 1635 Americans and their spouses (1078) who responded to an SRI International mail survey in 1980. VALS has had considerable impact since that time. Part of its allure comes from the vivid individual portraits that advocates paint of members of the various groups.

Need-Driven consumers exhibit spending by need rather than preference and are subdivided into survivors and sustainers, with the former among the most disadvantaged people in the economy. Outer-Directed consumers who are divided into three sub-groups, are the backbone of the marketplace and generally buy with awareness of what other people will attribute to their consumption of that product. Inner-Directed consumers are divided into three sub-groups. They comprise a much smaller percentage of the population. Their lives are directed more towards their individual needs than towards values oriented to externals. Although their numbers are small, they may be important as trend-setters or groups through whom successful ideas and products trickle up. This segment is growing rapidly, whereas the number of Need-Driven consumers is declining with Outer-Directed types holding steady.

The Need-Driven lifestyle

These people (11 per cent of the population) have values and life-styles which are very strongly affected by restrictions in money available to them. Their values tend to centre on the immediate and to focus on safety, security and survival. As consumers these people buy more from need than from choice and desire. Within this type, there are two specific market segments – 'Survivors' and 'Sustainers'.

Survivors are the very bottom of the hierarchy. This segment accounts for about 4 per cent of all adults. They are the most disadvantaged of Americans because of their older ages (average age is about 66 years), lower levels of education and income, and the lack of prospects for life to improve in the future. Many of the people in this segment lived most of their lives at higher levels of the VALS hierarchy, but now face a combination of economic and health problems that dominate their lives. The values of this group are traditional in nature. Minorities are over-represented in this group, as are women due to longer life expectancies.

Sustainers account for 7 per cent of the population. These people are much younger (average age 32) than the Survivor segment, but they also face economic restrictions that have a strong impact on their lives. This group also has low levels of education, and minorities are again over-represented. This group is at the edge of poverty, and its members' prospects of succeeding in the US economic system are not bright. Perhaps reflecting this, many members do not view the current socio-political system in a favourable light.

The Outer-Directed lifestyle

This segment (67 per cent of the population) represents the mainstream of the population, with two in three adults living in this lifestyle type. The outstanding characteristic of this type is that other people are used as guides for both values and behaviour. Concern for the social implications and norms of behaviour is quite high for all three segments here, although they differ from each other in some other important ways.

Belongers constitute the largest VALS segment with almost 40 per cent of the total population. They would rather 'fit in' than 'stand out'. These are the stabilisers of society, a strong force for traditional values and behaviour. Family, church and home are important to members of this segment. These individuals tend to be white, to be older than average and to have somewhat lower levels of education and income than most other segments.

Emulators are a much smaller (8 per cent of the population) and different group to Belongers. These people are young (average age 28) and are trying hard to 'make it big' in the system. They are ambitious, competitive and status conscious. Their lifestyles and values systems reflect (emulate) their aspirational reference group – the Achievers. Minorities are over-represented in this segment, the educational level is about average for all segments and the income level is above that of Belongers but below that of Achievers.

Achievers account for one-fifth of the population and include the leaders in business, the professions and government. These people are competent, successful and hard-working. They tend to have materialistic values, are pleased with the economic system and appear to be well satisfied with their place in society. Males are over-represented in this group and minorities are quite under-represented. Members are slightly older than average, have almost two years of college on average and hold the highest family income level of any segment.

The Inner-Directed lifestyles

The primary distinction between this lifestyle (making up 20 per cent of the population) and the outer-directed majority lies in the fact that these people seem more concerned with resolving issues in their inner lives than in dealing with the values of the external world. This does not mean that these people have rejected the lifestyles or value systems of the outer-directed. Instead, many of the people living in this lifestyle have been sufficiently successful that they have now chosen to pursue additional interests to that of economic success within the system.

I-Am-Me's are individuals in a transition stage that lasts only for a few years and represents a mix of values from both inner- and outer-directed lifestyles. This is a very small segment (only 3 per cent of the population), but an interesting one through which many people pass. The average I-Am-Me is 20 years old, has slightly less than a high school degree (though many are still in college) and has lower than average income (again as a result of the age of the group). People at this stage are fiercely individualistic, somewhat narcissistic and some-what exhibitionistic. As they are very concerned with their inner identities and external potentials, they are often willing to try new activities, to take risks and to act impulsively.

Experientials constitute another small segment (6 per cent of the population) which is also somewhat tied to a person's progress through the life cycle. Their average age is 26, they tend to be female and white, with higher than average educational levels and household incomes. This group is the most inner-directed of any of the segments and seeks personal involvement and experience with many aspects of life.

Societally conscious individuals represent the farthest step along the VALS inner-directed path and constitute 11 per cent of the adult population. These people have extended their value system beyond themselves to include various concerns with improving (as they see it) society as a whole. This is undertaken not for personal gain in a materialistic sense, but because the person believes that 'the world ought to be better than it is'. Many of these individuals support causes such as conservation, and many engage in extensive volunteer work. These individuals tend to be in their late-30s on average and have high levels of education and income.

The Integrated lifestyle

These are the rare 'self-actualising' individuals (2 per cent of the population) who represent the highest stage of the VALS system. Their values and lifestyles combine the power of the outer-directed achiever with the sensitivity of the inner-directed, socially conscious individual. They are 40 years old on average, hold a college degree and have a high income level. Because they account for only 2 per cent of the population, however, they are not a very significant segment for marketers aiming at the mass consumer market.

Do VALS segments differ in their consumerism?

It is worth taking a look at an illustration of the discriminative capability of VALS to segment consumer markets. Table 4.4 is taken from a publication by SRI and summarises data on six consumer markets. It can be seen that the imported wine market is highly segmented. Survivors virtually never buy this product (they may instead drink domestic wines or not drink much wines at all) and the other segments at the top of the list are also buying imported wines at rates much below the national average. The segments towards the bottom of the list constitute the 'heavy users' of imported wines. Since Belongers are by far the largest segment, marketers might in this case want to key in on this group to gain increased sales in the future.

The second column indicates the way in which competition occurs within a general use category. Notice that most segments buy cold cereals at about the national average, with Survivors and Emulators being lower, and the huge Belonger segment providing a massive sales base as they buy at higher than average rates.

The media columns show that it is possible to use VALS to segment markets according to their use of media. This is important in the context of planning media campaigns and knowing where the best media outlets are to place commercial messages in order to reach target markets. The example in the table shows how highly segmented the audiences are for TV comedy shows. The same is also true of sports magazine readerships. The final two columns indicate that VALS has been used to segment individuals on the basis of their activity and interest characteristics.

Table 4.4 VALS segments and consumer behaviour

| | Index of purchase/usage (national average rate = 1.0) | | | | | |
| | Products | | Media | | Activities | |
	Imported wine	Cold cereals	TV comedy	General sports magazines	Fishing	Museums/ galleries
Survivors (4%)	L(0.6)	L(0.8)	L(0.7)	L(0.0)	L(0.5)	L(0.4)
Sustainers (7%)	L(0.4)	–	H(2.0)	L(0.8)	H(2.0)	L(0.5)
Belongers (39%)	L(0.6)	H(1.3)	–	L(0.7)	H(1.3)	L(0.8)
Emulators (8%)	L(0.7)	L(0.7)	H(1.5)	H(1.2)	–	L(0.6)
Achievers (20%)	H(1.4)	–	L(0.7)	–	–	H(1.7)
I-Am-Me's (3%)	–	–	H(1.8)	H(2.0)	–	L(0.7)
Experientials (6%)	H(2.2)	–	H(1.4)	H(1.3)	–	H(1.3)
Societally conscious (11%)	H(1.9)	–	L(0.7)	–	L(0.7)	H(1.9)

Note: To be read 'Survivors drink imported wine at a much lower (L) than average rate, only 0.6 of the national average. Sustainers, Belongers and Emulators also buy imported wines at lower than average rates, while Achievers, Experientials and Societally conscious buy at higher (H) rates than the average. The I-Am-Me segment purchases imported wine at a rate close to the average (–)'.
Source: T. C. Thomas and S. Crocker (1981) *Values and Lifestyles – The New Psychographics*, Menlo Park, Calif. SRI International. Reproduced by permission of the publisher.

A COMPARISON OF VALS AND OTHER MONITORS

Research carried out in South Africa investigated a number of models of value typology including Mitchell's (1983) Values and Lifestyle (VALS), Market Research Africa's Sociomonitor (Corder, 1984) and Young and Rubicam's 4Cs model (Halley-Wright, 1988). Over-lapping categories were found in all of them. For instance, profile descriptions for survivors and sustainers in the VALS model corres-ponded with traditionals and responsibles in Sociomonitor, and with resigned and struggling poor in the 4C model (Rousseau, 1990). All these models are grounded in Maslow's (1954) need hierarchy, suggesting that certain goals, motivations and values are so basic that they are shared across the globe. According to Rousseau, the models are, therefore, primarily concerned with describing fundamental commonalities of the human psyche which transcend cultural, ethnic and national boundaries, and which work to predict lifestyle and purchase behaviour.

In South Africa, Sociomonitor focused on only three main sectors of Mitchell's hierarchy (need-driven, outer-directed and inner-directed) in analysing value systems and social change. For white South Africans, four value and lifestyle groups were identified. 'Responsibles' were older people characterised by conservation. They came from lower-income households and were concerned about security and provision for the future. Their self-confidence was weak and they constantly sought reassurance from others that what they were doing was acceptable. The 'Branded' group represented consumers who were often materially and educationally deprived. They strove for material possessions which would bring a sense of esteem, status and identity. How others saw and reacted to them was of major importance. 'Self-motivated' normally had post-matriculation qualifications, were affluent and had the insight to strive towards an inner-directed lifestyle. These people were individualistic, desired personal growth and held an aesthetic cultural outlook. 'Innovators' were well educated and consequently affluent. They combined outer and inner-directed values, and were on their way up the social and economic ladders. They tended to reject authority and the establishment, paid little attention to accepted social norms and were free thinkers and reformers who believed in changing society (Blem, Reekie and Brits, 1989).

For black South Africans, Sociomonitor identified five main groups in 1985. 'Traditionals' had a high regard for traditional black culture and heritage. They tended to be older, illiterate, conservative and very religious. 'Responsibles' were blue-collar workers who thought of the needs of others and felt strongly about the improvement of conditions for blacks generally. They wanted to ensure that their children were provided with more education and opportunities than they had. 'Brandeds' tended to live for today because of a general feeling of hopelessness. Group pressures were strong, they relied heavily on stimulants, and aggression and violence were an integral part of their lifestyle. 'I-Am-Me's' were a youthful group whose members were likely to portray a somewhat aggressive, swaggering self-confidence. The key trend was rejection of authority. They were firm believers in male superiority and were insensitive to the feelings and needs of others. 'Self-motivateds' were an 'elite group' in black society. They tended to be better educated, young, self-confident and ambitious. They were prepared to work harder to improve their qualifications, thereby improving their job opportunities (Blem, Reekie and Brits, 1989).

In testing a new integrated model of values and lifestyles among samples of white and black households in South Africa, Rousseau (1990) identified four lifestyle groups to provide a psychographic segmentation for furniture buyers. This model was built upon dimensions acquired from Maslow's need hierarchy, Mitchell's VALS, Market Research Africa's Sociomonitor and Young and Rubicam's 4Cs model. The model portrayed five hypothetical, consumer types; namely, Home-centred, Outer-directed, Trend-setters, Inner-directed and Cultured.

While based on general systems of values and lifestyle measurement, the model was product-specific in the sense that it focused upon furniture, and included hypothetical consumer types such as Home-centred, Trend-setters and Cultured which were related particularly to furniture buyers. According to Rousseau, it was unique to the furniture trade in that it augmented the outer and inner-directed value segments with an intervening stage, Trend-setters, in which fashion values dominated. The model further differed from Sociomonitor's typologies in that it included a hypothetical segment 'Cultured', which represented an integration of outer and inner-directed values in an elegant lifestyle. The model was a departure from usual psychographics systems in that as well as containing general lifestyle dimensions, it also included product and consumption-specific values.

NEW VALS SYSTEM

Riche (1989) reported on the new VALS system developed by SRI International. The first system was changed because its segments reflected a population dominated by people in their twenties and thirties, as the USA had been ten years earlier. Moreover, businesses found it difficult to use the segments to predict buying behaviour of target consumers.

For these reasons, SRI developed an all-new system. It dropped values and lifestyles as the basis for its psychographic segmentation scheme because the link between values and lifestyles, and purchasing choice seemed less strong than it had been. SRI attributed this change to several demographic and economical shifts: the ageing of the baby boom, the increasing diversity of the population, the rise of the global economy and the decline in consumers' expectations for the future. Combined with the increasing diversity of products, distribution and of media, values and lifestyles had become too fragmented to predict consumer behaviour.

The new system is based on a questionnaire that reveals

unchanging psychological stances rather than shifting values and life-styles. Instead of asking people about their attitudes to abortion or legalising marijuana, the new questionnaire asks them to agree or disagree with questions ranging from 'My idea of fun at a national park would be to stay in an expensive lodge and dress up for dinner', to 'I could stand to skin a dead animal'. The 43 questions are products of two nationally representative surveys of 2500 people SRI conducted in 1990. SRI did the first survey to develop the segmentation system, and the second to validate it and link it to buying and media behaviour.

VALS2

The psychographic groups in VALS2 are arranged in a rectangle. They are stacked vertically by their resources (minimal to abundant), and horizontally by their self-orientation (principle, status or action oriented). Resources include income, education, self-confidence, health, eagerness to buy, intelligence and energy level. Most resources tend to increase from youth through middle age, then diminish with old age. The oldest psychographic segment is the one on the bottom – Strugglers – with a median age of 61.

The self-orientation dimension captures three different ways of buying. Principle-oriented consumers are guided by their views of how the world is or should be; status-oriented consumers by the actions and opinions of others; and action-oriented consumers by a desire for social or physical activity, variety and risk taking.

Each of these orientations has two psychographic segments, one with high and one with low resources. The two principle-oriented segments are Fulfilleds and Believers. *Fulfilleds* are mature, respon-sible, well-educated professionals. Their leisure activities centre on their homes, but they are well-informed about what goes on in the world, and they are open to new ideas and social change. They have high incomes, but they are practical, value-oriented consumers. *Believers* have more modest incomes; they are conservative and predictable consumers who favour American products and estab-lished brands. Their lives are centred on family, church, community and the nation.

The two status-oriented segments are Achievers and Strivers. *Achievers* are successful, work-oriented people who get their satis-faction from their jobs and families. They are politically conservative, and respect authority and the status quo. They favour established products and services that show off their success to their peers.

Strivers have similar values but fewer resources – economic, social and psychological. Style is extremely important to them as they strive to emulate the people they wish they were.

The two action-oriented consumers are Experiencers and Makers. They 'like to affect their environment in tangible ways', according to SRI. *Experiencers* are the youngest of all the segments, with a median age of 25. They have a lot of energy, which they pour into physical exercise and social activities. They are avid consumers spending heavily on clothing, fast food, music and other youthful favourites – with particular emphasis on the new. In contrast, *Makers* are practical people who value self-sufficiency. They are focused on the familiar – family, work and physical recreation – and have little interest in the broader world. As consumers 'they are unimpressed by material possessions other than those with a practical or functional purpose'.

Strugglers have the lowest incomes and too few resources to be included in any consumer self-orientation. They are located below the rectangle. Within their limited means, they tend to be brand-loyal consumers. *Actualisers* have the highest incomes and such high self-esteem and abundant resources that they can indulge in any or all self-orientations. They are located above the rectangle. Image is important to them 'not as evidence of status or power, but as an expression of their taste, independence, and character', according to SRI. Because of their wide range of interests and openness to change, their consumer choices are directed toward 'the finer things in life'.

Unlike those of the first version of VALS, VALS2's segments are roughly equal in size. The group at the top of the old pyramid – the Integrateds – accounted for less than 2 per cent of the population. In VALS2, the smallest segment – the Actualisers – accounted for 8 per cent of the population. The other segments each represent from 11 to 16 per cent of the population.

SOCIAL VALUE GROUPS

Seven social value groups have been produced from research marketed by UK market research agency, Taylor Nelson Ltd. This monitor system is based on clusters derived from a data bank of more than 15 000 interviews conducted in the UK since 1973. The main instrument comprises nearly 160 items which measure 37 social trends.

The main purpose behind the Monitor system is to help companies respond to the general changes in social values that are taking place across any given period of time. Their repeated use over many years has enabled this system to be used as a source of values trends which can be applied to long-range planning and market forecasting, as well as for brand positioning at any particular point in time. The social value instrument has also been applied in the sphere of company audits of personnel values as a basis for defining the corporate culture and the measurement of employee attitudes towards different aspects of their organisation. The seven clusters are as follows.

Self-Explorer: Youthful, independent, comfortably situated, often female. These are self-aware people who cannot tolerate restriction unless self-imposed. They are confident, tolerant, imaginative and enjoy a secure, comfortable self-oriented lifestyle.

Social Register: An older group who resist change and seek to maintain the status quo. They have a high need for control over the self, family, community and society. They tend to seek to preserve traditional ethical and moral codes.

Experimentalist: Tend to be men in their late twenties or early thirties, independent and unconventional, and always looking for something new and different. They are energetic, confident, gregarious and intelligent, and work oriented.

Conspicuous Consumer: These are predominantly female office workers or housewives with a standard basic education. Essentially conformist with little need for personal satisfaction, their energy is directed towards romantic goals and material possessions. They generally lack self-confidence and mix with similarly oriented friends.

Belonger: Mature, stable and settled; the most married group of all and likely to have a young family. They place great store by the home, family, country, establishment and fair play.

Survivor: Tend to be male, unskilled or skilled manual workers, dependent on the protection of authority while also sceptical of its intentions. These people identify with the country, family and trade unions or a political party. They are motivated by basic physical and emotional needs.

Aimless: Lack orientation within society; goalless, uninvolved and alienated. Can be aggressive and resentful towards a system's authority. Unhappy and unable to improve their position, may turn to fantasy and cheap 'kicks' for distraction.

LIST OF VALUES

One alternative to VALS is the List of Values (LOV), which was developed by researchers at the University of Michigan Survey Research Centre (Kahle, 1983; Veroff, Douvan and Kulka, 1981).

LOV was developed from a theoretical base of Feather's (1975), Maslow's (1954) and Rokeach's (1973) work on values in order to assess adaptation to various roles through value fulfilment. It is tied most closely to social adaptation theory (Kahle, 1983, 1984). Subjects see a list of nine values, including self-respect, security, warm relationships with others, sense of accomplishment, self-fulfilment, sense of belonging, being well-respected, fun and enjoyment in life and excitement.

These values can be used to classify people on Maslow's (1954) hierarchy, and they relate more closely to the values of life's major roles (i.e., marriage, parenting, work, leisure, daily consumption), than do the values in the Rokeach (1973) Value Survey (Beatty *et al.*, 1985). In the LOV method, subjects have been asked to identify their two most important values (Kahle, 1983; Veroff *et al.*, 1981) or to rank the values (Beatty *et al.*, 1985) as Rokeach (1973) prefers with his value survey. The values could also be evaluated through paired comparison (Reynolds and Jolly, 1980) or rating (Munson, 1984) approaches.

The major study of these LOV values was a face-to-face survey of a probability sample of 2264 Americans conducted by the survey research centre in the Institute for Social Research at the University of Michigan. LOV has been related to a number of important measures of mental health, well-being and adaptation to society, roles and self (Kahle, 1983), as well as geographic dispersement (Kahle, 1986).

VALS and LOV have several obvious similarities – for example, the VALS classification of achievers and the LOV classification of sense of accomplishment, or the VALS classification of belongers and the LOV classification of sense of belonging. In some instances the overlap seems logically unlikely, such as the VALS classification of self-respect, because the groups are semantically quite different.

Both methods have identified an inner–outer distinction. In VALS the distinction is called outer-directed *vs.* inner-directed, but it derives from Riesman *et al.*'s (1950) concept of 'other-directed' (Holman, 1984). The outer-directed groups include Achievers, Emulators and Belongers, while the inner-directed groups include the Societally conscious, Experientials and I-Am-Me. In the LOV research the distinction is between internal *vs.* external locus of control (Rotter, 1965); the external values include sense of belonging, being well-respected, and security, while the internal values include the rest. LOV theory also notes the importance of people in value fulfilment. Values can be fulfilled through interpersonal relationships (warm relationships with others, sense of belonging), personal factors (self-respect, being well-respected, self-fulfilment), or personal things (sense of accomplishment, security, excitement, fun and enjoyment in life).

Both techniques of measurement have been carefully considered within the context of lifespan developmental psychology. Whereas in VALS the individual is viewed as going from worse to better (e.g., integrated people are better than sustainers), within the LOV framework no such expectation exists. Kahle, Beatty and Homer (1986) compared and contrasted the VALS and LOV methods of segmenting consumer markets and found that the LOV method had certain advantages over VALS. Their results implied that LOV significantly predicted consumer behaviour brands more often than did VALS (35 users, 12 consumer items).

One advantage of LOV is that one obtains the demographic prediction separately, which implies that a researcher can more readily identify the source of influence. Another obvious advantage of LOV over VALS is that it is simple to administer. Finally, it is easier to preserve the exact phrase from a value survey in an advertisement with LOV than with VALS, thus limiting the potential for mistaken communication as research passes through the marketing system.

Perri (1990) conducted a survey among 400 shoppers at two shopping malls, using the LOV method of assessing consumers' psychological profiles. The LOV scale is composed of nine value items on which consumers select the value with which they most identify, including self-respect, security, warm relationships with others, sense of accomplishment, self-fulfilment, sense of belonging, being well-respected, fun and enjoyment, and excitement. The author found that LOV was simple to administer and was well received by respondents. Consumers who valued self-respect, being well-respected and a sense of belonging were more likely to purchase more health and beauty aids than those with other psychographic profiles.

Recently LOV has been critically appraised and found to lack the robustness suggested by its founders. Novak and MacEvoy (1990) conducted a replication comparison of the VALS instrument with the LOV instrument with a national probability sample of US consumers. The authors argued that the earlier superiority claimed for the LOV over VALS may have been due to the part played by a set of seven demographic items included with the values statements in the LOV.

Novak and MacEvoy examined the predictive capacity of LOV with and without demographic variables and compared it with VALS.

They found that the LOV with demographics was as predictive as VALS, but that the LOV minus the demographic items was less powerfully predictive than VALS. Indeed, when comparing the demographic items with the remaining LOV items, they found that the former were more predictive of consumer behaviour than the latter. Thus, much of the predictive power of the original LOV instrument may lie with the demographic component. They concluded that VALS may be preferred over LOV as a basis for market segmentation. VALS can stand alone without demographic variables, while LOV without demographic variables is significantly less predictive than VALS alone. The authors also pointed out that SRI International introduced VALS2 as a replacement for the original VALS system. There are many conceptual and practical differences between VALS and VALS2, and it is not possible to generalise their results for VALS to VALS2.

Research on both LOV and VALS should continue. Neither system can come even close to perfect prediction, implying that value research will probably not become the marketer's panacea. But both systems display some utility and both systems improve on ignorance.

CONCLUSION

Numerous different general psychographic systems have been developed. They differ in theoretical origin, country of development and number of categories specified. Clearly they cannot be equally efficient at segmentation. Each is a general non-brand or product-specific attempt to segment total markets.

The problem with VALS-type segmentations is that they provide target values but are easily stereotyped. Furthermore, being US-based it is not clear when used in Europe whether they are 'real' or a function of the questionnaire and statistical analysis approach. They tend to predict broad product category behaviour but not brands (Cooper, 1988). However, the quality and quantity of the evaluative evidence available makes it difficult to either defend or reject the use of these systems. Naturally users swear by it and non-users reject it, but there is insufficient, good empirical evidence to support either side.

5 Critique of psychographics

INTRODUCTION

Psychographics or 'lifestyle' measures have become a popular means of identifying consumers and describing their differences along psychological dimensions, which supersede traditional demographic variables. During the 1960s and 1970s in America, and the 1980s in Britain, psychographic segmentation received widespread prominence in advertising and marketing research centres. Such prominence developed from the recognition that important demographic distinctions simply do not exist in many product categories and even where they do, one cannot intelligently decide how to attract any particular market segment unless one knows why the distinctions exist.

In effect, it has been understood that to attract or motivate a particular group of consumers, it is necessary to know how they think and what their values and attitudes are as well as who they are in terms of the traditional demographic variables of age, sex, income, family life cycle and so on.

But many questions remain unanswered. For one, the very definition of 'psychographics' remains a controversial one. Some have used the term to refer to basic personality characteristics, such as aggression, anxiety, extroversion or masculinity, while some have applied it to lifestyle variables, such as community involvement, home entertainment, leisure activities and so forth. Others have preferred definitions involving attitudes, values and beliefs considered more directly pertinent to the particular product class or classes under study – i.e., nutritional or convenience concerns for food; performance or safety values for automobiles; or proneness to illness for drugs.

Finally, still others have given primary emphasis to the benefits individuals specify as most desirable in a particular product – for example, decay prevention, whiteness and taste in a toothpaste; strength, flavour and ease of administration in a cough remedy.

Related to this first question is a second one. Can one use a single set of psychographic variables to provide meaningful information for a number of diverse product categories? Restricting the definitions to basic personality or lifestyle characteristics implies that these will provide a useful basis for classification in a wide variety of applications. Using product-oriented or benefit variables implies the necessity of tailoring the psychographic involvement to an individual product, or at least to a class of products similar in nature. There is also a third question: to what extent psychographics have successfully identified meaningful segments in the market? As few studies have been made public, this remains highly difficult to assess.

Despite the promise that psychographics can provide a more comprehensive means of market segmentation, over the years there have been a number of problems and limitations with this approach. Some of these limitations cannot be easily overcome, but others would respond to the use of more systematic and rigorous research methods. In general, psychographics or lifestyle research is designed to account for unit of association (individual, family) differences in some kinds of behaviour which cannot be accounted for by physiological, demographic and socio-economic characteristics.

The kinds of behaviour one would like to predict with lifestyle or psychographic variables can serve as a framework for distinguishing between two polar approaches to this kind of market segmentation research: (1) the situation-specific approach which is managerial in nature and focuses on the prediction of product or media-related behaviour, and (2) the general approach which is more concerned with a broad understanding of consumer (or even non-consumer) aspects of social behaviour. The latter approach was dealt with in the previous chapter, while the former will be examined in more detail in later chapters.

GENERAL OR SPECIFIC?

Many company-sponsored studies that include lifestyle or psychographic variables focus on highly specific items – involving single product class needs, problems, benefits sought – that are thought to be associated with fairly narrowly defined classes of behaviour, e.g., what brands of cosmetics is most preferred? Other, more general studies have used large batteries of items that were thought to be relevant for predicting individual differences across a wide variety of behaviour. Other studies have included both specific and general lifestyle items.

For all this effort, however, relatively little appears to be known about the relationship between the more specific versus the more general lifestyle or psychographics items. General systems of values and lifestyles measurements make only broad statements about consumer behaviour and market movements, while systematic links between such measures and different product-specific activities remain to be developed.

THE PROS AND CONS OF PSYCHOGRAPHICS

Are psychographic studies useful? There is strong disagreement on this point. Some users have been pleased with the studies they have conducted and believe that psychographics represents a major break-through in consumer research. Others have been disappointed with their experiences with psychographics and believe it to be a waste of time and money. Some believe that product-specific psychographic studies are extremely valuable, but that general lifestyle studies are useless; while still others believe the precise opposite.

Critics of psychographics generally base their criticisms on the following points:

(1) The groups of consumers created by psychographic analysis overlap so much that they do not differentiate among consumer types.
(2) The length of many, if not most, psychographic studies precludes obtaining a probability sample: thus the findings are non-representative and cannot be projected onto population groups.
(3) Psychographic studies reveal nothing that shrewd marketing practitioners or creative advertising writers do not already know or could not figure out if they just bothered to think about it.
(4) Psychographics is just another gimmick that has a certain naive appeal but no real substance.

Devout users of psychographics generally support its value with the following arguments:

(1) Granted that life-cycle groups overlap substantially, the marginal differences that exist can still be useful because differences of only a couple of percentage points are routinely used in making marketing decisions.
(2) Psychographic studies provide insights into the behaviour of

consumers that cannot be obtained in any other way, and these studies often inspire concepts and ideas that substantially strengthen the marketing effort.

(3) Psychographics is a powerful selling tool in helping advertising agencies obtain clients and in helping marketing personnel sell their recommendations to corporate management.

Comprehensive reviews of psychographics and market segmentation research, such as *Lifestyle and Psychographics* edited by Wells (1974), and the special section on market segmentation research of the *Journal of Marketing Research*, edited by Wind (1978), have levelled the following conceptual and operational criticisms at psychographic research:

(1) The validity of market segmentation solutions cannot be ascertained because of the limited theory linking segmentation descriptors to the decisions of the firm (Pernica, 1974; Wells, 1975; Wind and Green, 1974).

(2) Segmentation descriptors which are chosen because they richly describe should not necessarily be expected to predict well (Wells, 1974).

(3) Lifestyle and psychographic dimensions may have added to the predictive ability of demographics, but their relationships with consumer behaviour have been far from impressive (Frank, Massy and Wind, 1972; Wells and Tigert, 1971).

(4) By attempting to analyse 'everything with everything', psychographic market segmentation practice is merely an exploratory first stage of the research process (Hustad and Pessemeier, 1974; Wind and Green, 1974).

(5) Because of limited theoretical development, psychographics research ignores the hierarchy of effects learning behaviour consumers go through in making decisions (Wind, 1978).

(6) Since adequate psychographic theory has not been developed, the selection of segmentation descriptors and scales is too often a 'fishing expedition' (Hustad and Pessemeier, 1974; Wind and Green, 1974).

In its defence, psychographics have been used frequently because of the rich descriptive detail they have provided corporate strategists for developing marketing strategies. Numerous testimonials exist attesting to how the descriptive detail of psychographic research enhanced development of corporate marketing strategy.

Unlike demographics, many social and psychological factors are difficult to measure, being somewhat subjective, usually based on the self-reports of consumers and sometimes hidden from view (to avoid embarrassment, protect privacy, convey an image and other reasons). In addition, there are still ongoing disputes over terminology, misuse of data and reliability.

One of the pioneers of this area of research, William D. Wells, highlighted the problems and limitations of this approach to market segmentation:

> From the speed with which psychographics have diffused through the marketing community, it seems obvious that they are perceived as meeting a keenly felt need. The problem now is not so much one of pioneering as it is one of sorting out the techniques that work best. As that process proceeds, it seems extremely likely that psychographic methods will gradually become more familiar and less controversial, and eventually will merge into the mainstream of marketing research.
>
> (Wells, 1975: 209)

APPRAISING PSYCHOGRAPHICS

Psychographic research, when done well, can be a valuable tool to marketers; but when done badly it can be an expensive and useless waste of time and resources. Critical questions about psychographics can be discussed under three major headings: (i) reliability; (ii) validity; and (iii) applications to real world marketing problems.

Reliability

The tendency of many investigators to make up their own measures has usually resulted in the validity and reliability of these instruments being ignored or untested. Reliability needs to be tested at a number of levels before full confidence can be gained in a psychographic instrument. Although the intuitive appeal of the psychographics concept is clear, the reliability of its use in marketing research and by marketing practitioners is less certain. A reliable measure will yield the same finding on repeated occasions if the phenomenon has not changed.

What sense of reliability is being referred to? One sense is the strict technical definition: freedom from random error. When assessing reliability, it is important to distinguish between two major uses for psychographic measurements. One is as a public opinion poll. An investigator might want to know, for example, how many people agree with: 'There should be a bottle of gin in every home', 'Television commercials put too much emphasis on sex', etc. When samples are of the size typically found in marketing surveys, random errors tend to cancel, and overall averages and percentages tend to be quite stable.

The other use of psychographics is in statistical relationships, either cross tabulations or 'predictions' of dependent variables. Reliability is particularly important in studies of relationships. However, the reliability of some psychographic measurements – especially some individual 'homemade' items – may well be low enough to put a rather severe limitation on the accuracy of 'prediction'.

One of the first studies to address the issue of the reliability of psychographic variables was conducted by Tigert (1969). Using a test–retest reliability analysis for 16 psychographic dimensions, he observed that 11 had a reliability of 0.70 or higher, and the lowest reliability coefficient for any dimension was 0.59. In a subsequent study, Bruno and Pessemeier (1972) found a median test–retest reliability coefficient of between 0.60 and 0.69 for psychographic items, and about 0.80 for multi-item scales. Elsewhere, lower reliability scores (0.40–0.60) were reported by Villani and Lehmann (1975).

The few researchers reporting the reliability of psychographic variables have generally applied reliability analysis at two levels: the aggregate level and the individual level. The aggregate or group marketing strategies are typically designed for groups. For example, decisions to segment markets must be based on an assumed degree of aggregate stability over a period of time. Alternatively, researchers concerned with individual level reliability are oriented towards different methodological phenomena and have a different interpretation of reliability. The presence of stochastic responses to psychographic instruments often causes individual level reliability to be below the aggregate level.

The apparent reliability of the phenomenon being measured would be also affected by any 'real' change in the individual between tests. In fact, a low test–retest reliability score would be expected on variables that have actually measured change. For this reason it is helpful to distinguish between psychographic variables that are more or less likely to change.

It is generally assumed, implicitly by many psychographic researchers, that people are consistent if asked the same set of questions a few months later, even though it is known from research in other areas of psychology that the answers to some questions are heavily dependent on a person's current mood. A few investigators, however, have explicitly distinguished lasting versus temporary individual characteristics. Thus, Tigert (1969) found that stable factors included psychographic characteristics of fashion consciousness, price or 'specials' shopping and weight watching. Unstable factors included new brand trier, brand loyalty and satisfaction with life and income. Some researchers have underlined the importance of distinguishing, at a conceptual level, between personal attributes that reflect responses to a particular set of circumstances or situations and personal enduring behaviour, which characterises individuals across a range of situations (Hustad and Pessemeier, 1974). This, clearly, is something which needs to be borne in mind when testing the stability and reliability of psychographic variables.

Burns and Harrison (1979) investigated the reliability of 36 items over a one-year period, and found that only 18 were used consistently. Of the remaining 18, 12 items appeared to reflect lasting personality characteristics, while 6 measured characteristics in which real change had occurred over the time period. The Burns and Harrison study illustrates the importance of allowing for real population changes in attitudes and lifestyles. Previous research into the characteristics of cigarette smokers, users of lead-free petrol or the buyers of certain types of car can easily be superseded by economic developments, such as the introduction of new taxation arrangements, that radically alter user profiles. These historical factors, however, are a problem with all methods of segmentation and are not confined to psychographics.

These results indicate that one needs to be cautious when interpreting reliability scores on psychographic instruments based on aggregated scores over a set of items. High reliability scores over a collection of items, when treated in an aggregated fashion, may disguise the fact that respondents' positions on certain individual items may have changed significantly. The conclusion is not entirely discouraging, however. When one inspects the degree of individual random response to items, most respondents appear to vary fairly unsystematically.

The specification of an acceptable level of reliability cannot be arbitrary. However, the user of psychographics must realise that an assessment of the stability of psychographic dimensions necessarily precedes the use of the individual psychographic items. Moreover, the user must realise that some dimensions are more reflective of lasting personal characteristics and behaviours and others are more likely to show the susceptibility and reactions of the individuals to external influences.

The maximum possible correlation between two variables is as fully dependent upon the reliability of what is being predicted as it is upon the reliability of the predictor. In psychographic studies, where the dependent variable is normally some form of consumer behaviour, this means that strong relationships cannot be obtained unless the consumer behaviour itself is measured accurately, no matter how reliable the psychographic measurements may be. For example, some kinds of consumer behaviour – such as choice of a specific brand on a given occasion of exposure to a particular television programme – may be so unstable that accurate prediction is virtually impossible, quite apart from any random measurement errors. Indeed Bass (1974) has gone so far as to assert that individual brand choice is so unstable that it can never be accurately predicted by psychographics or anything else.

With a few exceptions, psychographic researchers have not investigated the reliability of dependent predicted variables. Successful prediction implies (but does not certify) adequate reliability. But unsuccessful prediction can be due to unreliability in the psychological measurements, to unreliability in the dependent variables, to lack of any 'real' relationships between the psychographics and the behaviour in question, or to some combination of all three. In the absence of reliability data it is impossible to determine which is the case.

Closely related to the question of reliability of relationships is the question of reliability of structure: do psychographic variables relate to each other in much the same way from study to study? In their reliability review, Pessemeier and Bruno (1971) compared factor analysis results from five large scale studies, including one conducted in Canada. They concluded that 'the wide range of variables employed and the constructs to which they relate appear to be sufficiently reliable for both practical and theoretical purposes' (Pessemeier and Bruno, 1971: 397). This conclusion is encouraging because it asserts that items tend to cluster together in much the same way when studies are repeated. If that were not the case, it would be hard to put much credence in their relationship to anything else.

Validity

A measurement is 'valid' to the degree that it really does measure what it was intended to measure. This can be established by looking at how the items perform in independent samples, at their relationship to conceptually similar and distinct items, and at their ability to confirm prior predictions. Like other measurements, psychographic measurements can be reliable without being valid. They can be relatively free of random error but so full of irrelevances and biases that conclusions based on them are partly (or even completely) false.

The issue of the validity of lifestyle traits has been reviewed by Lastovicka (1982), who found only 14 attempts at validation despite the vast quantity of research carried out. In his own study, Lastovicka showed that it is possible to validate lifestyle traits, although not all traits will stand up to close scrutiny. Recent work on describing shopper types by means of psychographic profiles has confirmed that segmentations can show reasonable stability (reliability) across different geographical locations with different kinds of market (Lesser and Hughes, 1986). More attention needs to be paid to validation, particularly because many traits are only measured with a single item, and others are assessed with short scales consisting of heterogeneous items. Whether or not the items do measure the purported trait is too often taken for granted, without actually being proven.

The construct validity of a measurement is established by showing that it relates to those variables to which it should be related, and does not relate to other variables to which it should not be related. The process of establishing construct validity is normally spread out over time. It involves gradual accumulation of evidence, often by independent investigators, rather than being based on a single finding.

Pessemeier and Bruno's review of the stability of certain psychographic constructs (Bruno and Pessemeier, 1972; Pessemeier and Bruno, 1971) provides some evidence that bears upon the construct validity question. The fact that similar factors did indeed emerge when similar sets of items were answered by independent samples of respondents provides some assurance that individual psychographic items tend to relate to each other in consistent ways. Further evidence of construct validity can be found in the relationship between demographic and psychographic variables. The evidence is not always conclusive, but when young people differ from old people in expected ways, or when more college graduates that non-graduates agree with 'most of my friends have never had a college education' the responses to the psychographic items seem right.

Beyond such internal consistency, evidence for the construct validity of homemade items and scales is hard to find. The most general practice is to assume, unless there is evidence to the contrary, that the respondent is reporting accurately. Stated boldly, this assumption sounds naive, but it is common in marketing research. When respondents are asked about brand preferences, exposure to media or consumption of products, answers are taken at face value, even though it is known that such answers are sometimes wrong.

The psychographic researcher who uses standardised scales is less dependent upon face validity than is the researcher who assembles their own set of independent variables. Almost all published attitude scales and personality inventories are accompanied by at least some validity data, and some instruments are accompanied by quite a lot. If the scale has been widely used, the results of construct validity studies can be found in published academic reviews and other sources.

Regardless of how thoroughly validated a standardised scale has been in connection with the original clinical or academic context in which it was originally developed, marketing researchers need to give careful consideration to their reasons for using a particular scale as a predictor of consumer behaviour. Often this matter is not properly thought through and the scales may be inappropriately selected. Construct validity data need to be carefully interpreted so that the researcher can be confident that this is the scale for the occasion.

Marketing policy decisions should not be made lightly on the basis of market segments derived from psychographic instruments, whether they are homemade or standardised. If market segments have validity, then they ought to appear repeatedly and consistently across different samples to which the same marketing instrument is applied. If segments disappear or change dramatically in size from sample to sample, one must have severe doubts as to whether they represent 'real' sections of the population. But even when segments appear reliably across samples, this is not the end of the story. There must still be confidence that the descriptions allocated to each segment apply equally or sufficiently to each member of that group. A market segment could be described as 'outwardly directed', for example; but to what extent does this description apply to all respondents who fall within range?

In econometrics, the validity of a model is established by its ability to predict the summed or averaged behaviour of a large number of individuals. In psychometrics, the validity of a test is established by its ability to predict the behaviour of separate individuals. This distinction is important because the degree of accuracy that can be expected of predictions at the aggregate level is much higher than the degree of accuracy that can be expected of predictions at the individual level.

The results of individual level predictions with psychographic instruments have paralleled the experiences in research on personality. In the absence of good reason to believe that the psychographic construct would be closely related to the consumer behaviour being studied, correlations tend to be slightly higher (up to 0.30) than personality and demographic measures. Also when relevant dimensions have been linked together in multiple regression, multiple correlations have been in the 0.50–0.60 range.

Whether this record is good or bad depends greatly upon one's point of view. Many critics have declared that low correlations are not of practical value and have dismissed them out of hand. Others have argued that accounting for differences between groups, rather than explaining the variance in individual behaviour, is often the real object of psychographic analysis. From that standpoint the record looks much better.

APPLICATION OF PSYCHOGRAPHICS

One difficulty lies in the enormous range of questions to which psychographics is relevant. Some broad-based questions require segmentation into general types such as 'Achievers' or 'Emulators'. It is then hoped that the same fairly limited set of types can be used to explain many different kinds of consumer behaviour in widely different product areas. At the other extreme psychographics is called upon to describe the characteristics of people who behave in a highly specific way, such as buying brand X rather than the highly similar brand Y, or buying large versus small quantities of the same product. In these cases, few assumptions need be made about the generality of the traits being measured.

One consequence of this state of affairs is that a very great number of psychographic profiles have been generated, all based on different measures. Lastovicka (1982) noted over 100 lifestyle traits that had been used in different studies. Some of the lifestyle inventory measures are brief, containing only a dozen or so items, while others contain established questionnaires and may be based on hundreds of individual items. There has been little attempt to standardise items or concepts, with the result that the relation between all these various measures is unknown. Neither is there a recognised body of normative data with which to compare the results of individual surveys. This is obviously inefficient and a poor use of resources. Another major problem concerns the way in which psychographic profiles of different consumer types are drawn up. Often the sampling frame is inadequate, so that the generality of the types is likely to be limited. In extreme cases the typology is based on a small number of qualitative interviews, which cannot really be claimed to generate anything more than some hypotheses to be tested in subsequent quantitative research. One might as well simply make it all up on the back of an envelope! Even when quantitative methods have been used, however, insufficient attention is frequently paid to ensuring representative sampling of respondents.

The results of psychographic research can be reliable and valid, and yet still not useful when inadequately substantial hypotheses fail to be confirmed. This may seem like a perfectly obvious thing to say, yet the literature is full of attempts to predict consumer behaviour from personality test answers/scores in the absence of good reason to believe that the two should be related (Jacoby, 1971a).

Perhaps the classic 'shot in the dark' is an early psychographic effort in which scales from the Edwards Personal Preference Schedule – scales intended to measure such needs as autonomy, dominance, order and endurance – were correlated with purchases of single- and double-ply toilet tissue (Advertising Research Foundation, 1964). Even if it were true that all of the measurements in this study were perfectly reliable and perfectly valid, the failure to find significant correlations between the need for dominance or endurance and the purchase of toilet paper could hardly come as much of a surprise. The same general comment applies to Evans' (1959) finding that the Edwards scales could not separate Ford owners from Chevrolet owners; to Robertson and Myers' (1969) finding that California Personality Inventory scores did not account for much of the variance in innovativeness or opinion leadership; and to Kollat and Willett's (1960) finding that a set of general personality traits including optimism, belief in fate and belief in multiple causation of events, did not predict impulse purchasing.

Psychographic measurement may be reliable and valid but be so close to the behaviour being studied that the relationship is essentially redundant. To be useful in making real world decisions in marketing, psychographic data must lie in some middle range between being redundant and being unrelated to the behaviour being studied. They must contain just the right element of surprise. When that is the case they can indeed be useful, even when correlations are not high and even when questions about reliability and validity cannot be completely answered.

CONCLUSION

Perhaps the most serious problem with previous psychographic research is the absence of any theoretical rationale for the measures used. Often a standard personality questionnaire or set of lifestyle items is applied to a sample without any thought being given to the nature of consumer behaviour and the factors that are likely to be influential. Without a comprehensive model of personality, lifestyle and consumer behaviour, this hit-and-miss approach is likely to over-look many important variables. For example, those who first buy a product, those who continue to buy it, those who are highly satisfied with it, those who buy it in the greatest quantities, and those who show brand loyalty, may all have rather different motivations and psychographic profiles.

The reasons why people buy products are also enormously varied, and our review of personality and consumer behaviour identified a number of potentially important consumer characteristics that have hardly been investigated at all. So far there has been little attempt at a comprehensive formulation of the attitudes, values and lifestyle characteristics that are most widely applicable to consumer behaviour.

To sum up, this chapter has reviewed many of the problems with existing psychographic research, identifying: (a) too many unrelated measures; (b) inadequate sampling; (c) measures of unknown reliability and validity; (d) potentially important personality variables overlooked; (e) the lack of a coherent theoretical rationale; and (f) an insufficiently detailed analysis of consumer behaviour. Most of these problems are remediable, and there are examples of thoughtful psychographic research in the literature with a sound methodology and generating good insights. But these examples are at present in the minority; a fact that is preventing the most effective use of what are powerful tools for the understanding and solving of marketing problems.

Applications of psychographics: I. Consumer activity

INTRODUCTION

Psychographic methods have contributed to change the general knowledge on consumer behaviour in at least three ways:

(1) Psychographic profiles have shed new light on some of the familiar and recurring topics in consumer research;
(2) Trend data now becoming available have shown how consumers are changing and how they are not;
(3) Special segmentations of the consumer population have created new hypotheses by which consumer behaviour may be more efficiently described and better understood.

Profiles

Psychographic profiles have already contributed to our understanding of opinion leadership (King and Sprokes, 1973; Reynolds, 1972), innovativeness (Coney, 1972; Donnelly, 1970; Jacoby, 1971a; Tigert, 1969), private brand buying (Bunger and Schott, 1972), social class (Tigert and Wells, 1970), consumer activism (Hustad and Pessemeier, 1973), catalogue buying behaviour (Reynolds, 1974), differences between Canada and the United States (Arnold and Tigert, 1973), and concern for the environment (Kinnear, Taylor and Sadrudin, 1972, 1974).

Trend data

As studies are repeated over time it becomes possible to accumulate trend data that show how consumers are changing. Such data are particularly valuable in an era when every other observer is prepared to describe 'the changing consumer' and to make predictions about the effects of the changes upon markets for goods and services. In monitoring trends, the task of empirical psychographic analysis is to highlight the changes that are actually happening given the factors that are remaining stable (Carmen, 1974; Plummer, 1973).

New typologies

The third application of psychographics in the study of consumer behaviour is just beginning to take shape. General segmentations have begun to produce the outlines of a new consumer typology. As groupings are identified and confirmed by independent sets of investigators, it is at least possible that markets will begin to think similarly in terms of segments demarcated by common sets of activities, interests, needs and values, and to develop products, services and media schedules specifically to meet them.

Agreement about general segmentation has often been far from complete. Differences in item content, sampling procedures and analytic technique have produced different sets of findings each claiming to be valid. Yet even though segments produced by more general segmentation studies differ in a number of ways, there is enough similarity between them to suggest that currently a commonly agreed system or agreed set of dimensions will emerge.

Psychographic lifestyle profiles can provide both general and specific information about consumers' activities, interests and opinions across a range of experiences and issues. As already seen, psychographic profiling can be general in its frame of reference, or specific. In some studies, psychographic profiles are drawn from large data sets of general lifestyle statements to produce a typology which covers the whole consumer population. In such cases, if the list of items is diverse enough, the typology it yields will be related to a wide range of consumer product preferences and behaviours. Examples of this type of psychographic framework are VALS (Mitchell, 1983) and LOV (Kahle, Beatty and Homer, 1986).

Many psychographic studies are far less ambitious in their terms of reference and attempt to develop profiles which segment and describe the character of consumer markets for specified product categories or even for single products. When a psychographic study is devoted to a single product category, it is not necessary to depend on item diversity to the same extent to get useful and usable consumer types. It is essential though, to ensure that items that are used have been carefully selected so as to be relevant to the product under consideration.

The application of psychographic techniques to the study of consumerism has been extremely diversified. Psychographic profiles have been investigated in connection with a wide range of products, including take-away foods (Tigert, Lathrope and Bleeg, 1971), eye make-up, shortening, oranges and lemons (Wells and Tigert, 1971), heavy-duty hand soap (Plummer, 1971), bank charge cards (Plummer, 1971), department stores (Michaels, 1973) and air travel (Behaviour Science Corporation, 1972). They also include profiles of the readers of magazines (Roper, 1970; Tigert *et al.*, 1971). In all cases, the psychographic data have provided rich, descriptive detail that could not have been inferred from demographics alone.

In addition to profiles of consumers in relation to their preference for, or use of, particular products, psychographics has been used to produce segmentation of population sub-groups such as women, the elderly or young professional people. It is worth looking in more detail at some of these applications to illustrate the way in which psychographics has been utilised in market segmentation research.

Earlier chapters have examined research into the application of standardised personality tests and custom-built psychographics' instruments to provide general and product-specific psychological profiles of consumer populations. Attempts to produce broad psychographic systems covering the consumer universe for example, have resulted in a number of syndicated market segmenting services. SRI's VALS programme (Values and Lifestyles) categorises people based on attitudes, needs, wants and beliefs. This and other similarly syndicated services such as The Monitor and Target Group Index are becoming increasingly popular. VALS and Monitor offer pre-developed consumer types, while TGI provides a more flexible system from which clients can define their own types based on selected clusters of attitudinal items.

There is, however, some question as to the effectiveness of syndicated psychographics. This form of generalised lifestyle research is market or consumer-driven as opposed to product-driven. This is perhaps less true of TGI than of the others offering already established consumer types. Individuals are analysed as to their overall attitudes, values and desires. Product-specific data – more significant information from a market segmentation perspective – are not obtained. Marketers can only infer how consumer segments will respond to their product offerings. Ideally, marketing planners would want to know this information. Since customers react differently when exposed to alternative product stimuli, the need for situation-specific data focusing on unique markets, product classes and product items is paramount.

It can be more useful therefore to apply psychographics in the context of profiling consumers in specific product or service categories. This chapter reviews research which has done just that. While earlier chapters focused on the various psychological classifications deriving either from personality theories or specifically developed measures of consumer lifestyles, the spotlight is now turned on the product end of the equation. The areas covered are general and specific categories of consumer activity, covering broad shopping behaviours and psychographic studies of consumers for specific products.

SHOPPING TYPES

It is important for retailers to have a thorough understanding of their consumers. The ability to classify consumers into relevant market segments can guide the way stores are designed and located, and inform communication and promotional campaigns aimed at building consumer awareness of the business and shaping the right sort of store image. Understanding not only what customers need, but also how they think and feel about shopping is essential in today's increasingly competitive retail environment if businesses are to maintain their market share.

In the past, demographic characteristics of consumers have generally been found useful both for selecting media and designing store atmospheres when variations in clientele are small. In addition, demographic dimensions were found, for example, to differentiate between segments of food shoppers, while specific retail shopping sub-segments, such as the in-home shopper, have been found to possess unique demographic profiles (e.g., higher income and educational levels) (Sexton, 1974). Combinations of socio-economic characteristics (e.g., income and social class) have also significantly contributed to the explanation of patronage decisions between discount and department stores across particular product categories (Prasad, 1975).

Demographic segmentations, however, provide relatively hollow classifications of consumers. For instance, they reveal nothing about the motives of consumers which underlie their decisions about when and where to shop, particularly where specific kinds of items are concerned. Research confirms lifestyle analysis as a useful method for identifying shopper communication needs and designing viable retailing promotional strategies based upon shopping orientations (Moschis, 1976). Psychographic descriptions have also been useful in explaining patronage preferences for retail store attributes and in examining behavioural correlates of the generalised store-loyal consumers (Darden and Ashton, 1974).

The pioneering study of shopping orientations was conducted by Stone (1954), who suggested that the more meaningful determinants of shopping behaviours are social–psychological in origin. Darden and Reynolds (1971) surveyed 200 housewives about their shopping attitudes and behaviour. Four major shopping types were identified, which supported the shopping orientations identified by Stone. These shopper types were then used to distinguish usage rates for a range of health and personal care products. Usage rates for roll-on or stick deodorant, liquid face make-up base and medicated face make-up base were related most powerfully to shopping orientations. Usage rates for products such as hand lotion, eye make-up and deodorants exhibited much less association with particular shopper types. The four shopping orientations were labelled:

(1) Economic shopper;
(2) Personalising shopper;
(3) Apathetic shopper;
(4) Ethical consumer.

The *Economic shopper* tended to be socially mobile and aspiring. The profile suggested a consumer who is concerned with price, quality and convenience, and who has impersonal relations with both local and larger chain stores. Economic shoppers exhibited high usage rates for products which are socially visible or produce socially visible effects, such as liquid face make-up base, medicated face make-up base, hand cream and hair spray.

The *Personalising shopper* tends to prefer small local shops over large, impersonal department stores. This type of consumer may develop 'quasi-personal' relationships with the people who work in local shops. This consumer does not shop as often for the more socially visible products however, and this may reflect a limited social life. Personalising shoppers had high usage rates for hair shampoo, roll-on or stick deodorant and cleansing face cream or lotion.

The *Apathetic shopper* represents the consumer who does not like to shop and who has no special loyalty to any kind of retail outlet. This consumer type finds no satisfaction in establishing personal relations with local shops and feels no emotional ties towards the local retail establishment. Apathetic shoppers were found to use a lot of medicated face make-up base, hair shampoo and, to a lesser extent, roll-on or stick deodorant and hand lotion.

The *Ethical shopper* exhibited strong, loyal support for the local shopkeeper. These consumers tend to be of high social status and to have lived in their local community for a long time. They believe chain stores to be a threat to the local store, and in particular to the highly-valued relationships they have often built up between themselves and local shopkeepers. This type of consumer had a high usage rate for cleansing face cream and lotion, hair spray and cream deodorant.

The categories may or may not be useful for marketers. Certainly shops as much as shoppers could be categorised by the same taxonomy. However, what remains unclear, and quite fascinating, is why these different shoppers have quite different buying preferences and habits.

THE SUPERMARKET CUSTOMER

American research among shoppers has attempted to identify if there are distinct psychological types who use supermarkets. There are two principal questions on this subject. First, are there groups of shoppers who exhibit distinct preferences for supermarket shopping? Second, do different supermarket shoppers have distinct lifestyle characteristics? Darden and Ashton (1974) interviewed 116 suburban housewives about their shopping habits; in particular, questions regarding what they liked about supermarkets. Seven distinct shopping types emerged:

(1) *Apathetic shopper* (22 per cent of the sample) did not express any particular preferences for shopping in supermarkets, with two exceptions. Sixty per cent of this sub-section demanded competitive prices and 52 per cent preferred supermarkets with a wide brand variety.
(2) *Demanding shopper* (8.6 per cent) demanded excellence all round, although they were not particularly concerned about trading stamps. They liked clean supermarkets with friendly personnel at convenient locations; they expected wide brand variety with quality meat cuts.
(3) *Quality shopper* (19 per cent) demanded fresh produce and quality meat cuts. They did not expect much more than this from a supermarket.
(4) *Fastidious shopper* (15 per cent) preferred supermarkets with

spick-and-span facilities. They also expected a wide assortment of brands for all products.

(5) *Stamp Preferred shopper* (12 per cent) comprised those preferring supermarkets offering trading stamps (or some equivalent). A majority among this group also expect quality products, competitive prices, brand variety, friendly sales assistants and clean stores.

(6) *Convenient Location shopper* (14.7 per cent) required only one attribute of a supermarket; that it be conveniently located.

(7) *Stamp Haters* (8 per cent) actually preferred stores not offering trading stamps. Other than this negative preference, these consumers had preference profiles resembling those of the total sample.

The authors of this research are cautious about generalising from their results too far. They wisely suggest that the idea behind their research could provide a framework for the study of psychographic profiles in other trading areas. It is expected that these other areas would have unique supermarket attribute preference groups. The percentage distribution and preference attributes of these groups can be valuable input for planning the supermarket mix.

There is less evidence pertaining to the second question. However, it seems likely that the lifestyles and shopping orientation of each group can be valuable input for understanding and influencing supermarket patronage in an area. Promotion, for example, can be enhanced by understanding the shopping predispositions of high potential retail preference groups. By understanding the patronage target, through an analysis of customer lifestyles, selection of the product mix should be improved.

Are psychographic profiles generalisable across different geographic markets? This question has been explored among shopper types. Lesser and Hughes (1986) used a psychographic inventory which comprised 34 statements reflecting general lifestyle activities and consumer shopping orientations (store benefits and shopping information sources). Altogether the inventory represented the following dimensions: price consciousness, interest in private brands, shopping information of shopping convenience, interest in outdoor activities, tendency to be a do-it-yourself type, propensity to try new products and tendency to make impulse purchases. Seven shopper types were discovered: *Inactive* shoppers (15 per cent of all shoppers), *Active* shoppers (12.8 per cent), *Service* shoppers (10 per cent), *Traditional* shoppers (14.1 per cent), *Dedicated Fringe* shoppers (8.8 per cent), *Price* shoppers (10.4 per cent) and *Transitional* shoppers (6.9 per cent). The most promising result was the considerable degree of similarity in types yielded across 17 geographic markets, indicating that the psychographic segments developed in one geographic market may be generalisable to other geographic markets.

Lesser and Hughes (1986) claim that the 'substantiality' of market segmentation, based on psychographics, as a frame of reference is supported. This suggests that retail businesses may confidently attempt to develop systematic, carefully targeted marketing strategies that appeal to 'basic' consumer segments existing in every geographic market.

PSYCHOGRAPHIC PROFILES FOR DIFFERENT RETAIL CATEGORIES

One of the major problems with research into shopper types is whether they can be generalised across different markets or specific to particular areas of retailing. On this question there is conflicting evidence. A good deal of the research into retail market segmentation has classified consumers arbitrarily across situations and competitive environments (Samli, 1975). There is a need to establish, for instance, whether along with the most fundamental segmentation dimension – patronage versus non-patronage – the distinguishing characteristics of these two groups exhibit any consistency in respect of different types of retail business. To identify and attract potential consumers, retail businesses must determine how patrons differ from non-patrons.

One study examined demographic, psychographic and media consumption differences between customers and non-customers of four types of retail outlet: convenience store, department store, discount store and fast food franchise (Bearden, Teel and Durand, 1978). Unique and statistically significant differences were found between customers and non-customers for each retailing category. There were, in particular, a few variations in the way that psychographic dimensions distinguished customers from non-customers in each retailing context. Five psychographic dimensions were identified from an original set of 29 opinion statements. These types, with sample statements in parentheses, were:

(1) *Traditionalist* ('I have some old-fashioned tastes and habits');
(2) *Outgoing/Individualist* ('I would rather fix something myself than take it to an expert');
(3) *Quality service* ('I will go out of my way to find a bank with good service');

(4) *Socially conscious* ('If my clothes are not in fashion, it really bothers me');
(5) *Other-directed* ('I usually ask for help from other people in making decisions').

Comparisons of customers and non-customers of convenience and department stores produced the most consistently significant differences. Convenience food store shoppers tended to be younger, to be male, to be better educated, to earn more and to be consistently heavier users of all media than non-customers. Convenience shoppers also differed from others in being less traditional, less outgoing and less socially conscious. Customers of department stores were found to be more quality conscious and more outer-directed than non-customers.

Unique differences were also found for the remaining two retail categories. While discount store customers were again younger and better educated than non-customers, their average income was less. The discount store shopper was also found to be less outgoing, less traditional and generally more socially conscious than non-customers. Less variation in media consumption patterns was found for discount shopper segments than for other retail categories. Users of fast food outlets might be uniquely described as younger, better educated and earning more than non-users. Fast food users were also found to be more outgoing, more socially conscious and heavier consumers of local media than were non-users.

A more direct comparison of department and discount retailers revealed that although both patronage groups possessed remarkably similar demographic profiles, the department store shopper was generally a heavier consumer of media, more concerned with quality, less outgoing and more socially conscious than the discount store shopper. Based on the results of this study, a word of caution is offered to retailers about the generalisability of psychographic segmentation across different types of retail business.

Psychographic descriptions of consumers can provide useful information in developing store image, both through the interior design of outlets and in advertising campaigns. However, the psychographic profile for one type of retail institution does not necessarily provide conclusive and valuable information for managers of other retail institutions. Substantial differences between patrons of different retail establishments indicate that segmentation results appear to be domain (retail institution) specific.

LOCAL VERSUS NON-LOCAL SHOPPING

One important feature of shopping behaviour is the extent to which shoppers rely mainly on shops in their own locality or are motivated and prepared to travel outside their area to buy the things they want. Marketing researchers have long been interested in spatial aspects of consumer shopping behaviour, and the origin of most studies in this field can be traced to early work in retail gravitation (Converse, 1949; Reilly, 1953).

These pioneering studies made significant contributions to marketing research and practice; although they require relatively simple data (market size and distance), they provide an accurate determination of the geographic boundaries of a market area. When it became clear that distinct market areas could be defined (Bucklin, 1971; Huff, 1964), researchers began to evaluate more precisely the impact of other factors on consumer patronage patterns within the boundaries of the market (Bucklin, 1966, 1967; Dommermuth and Cundiff, 1967; Haines, Simon and Alexis, 1971; Moore and Mason, 1969). The focus of most of these studies was on characteristics of the market, rather than characteristics of the consumer.

Research elsewhere, however, has indicated that much shopping takes place outside the local trade area (Herman and Beik, 1963; Thompson, 1971). Such movements of shoppers are especially important in terms of competition: retailers in a major urban shopping centre would like to attract shoppers from far afield, and, conversely, local store owners would like to keep customers from going elsewhere to do their shopping. To develop attractive merchandising strategies, retailers need to know more about the 'outshopping' segment of the market. Just who are the loyal, local shoppers and who are the ones who are prepared to travel miles?

Shopping outside the local trade area can be expensive in terms of transportation, energy, time and money. Nevertheless, it seems that some consumers prefer to travel outside their own locale to obtain the items they want. Poor selections and offerings locally may motivate this behaviour. However, some people are simply more adventurous or need more variety and choice than others. Hence, they can be prepared to go out of their way to get what they want. A number of exploratory studies have been carried out with the aim of identifying the individual consumer characteristics of outshoppers and inshoppers. One finding is that outshoppers are younger and better educated, have higher incomes and fewer children (Herman and Beik, 1963; Thompson, 1971). From this early research, market characteristics such as superior selections and fashion offerings, and a wide choice and variety of products and brands outside the local area, were identified as primary reasons for outshopping. In addition, it has been found that outshoppers are more gregarious, active and flexible compared to inshoppers (Reynolds and Darden, 1972b).

Darden and Perreault (1976) investigated the consumer and lifestyle characteristics of people who shop predominantly in their local trade area (inshoppers) versus those who make frequent shopping trips further afield (outshoppers). They completed personal interviews with more than 300 suburban housewives in a medium size city of 80 000 population in the state of Georgia, USA. Information was obtained from these women about the extent to which they shopped inside or outside the home trading area for 13 different kinds of commodity. From these data, respondents were divided into five different shopper types: Inshoppers, Big-ticket Outshoppers, Furniture Outshoppers, Appearance Outshoppers and Home Entertainment Outshoppers.

Inshoppers shopped predominantly in the home trading area for all product categories. *Big-ticket Outshoppers* travelled outside their own locality for expensive home products (home accessories, sporting goods, major appliances and small appliances). *Furniture Outshoppers* are self-explanatory. *Appearance Outshoppers* went outside their own area for jewellery and women's and men's apparel. Finally, *Entertainment Outshoppers* visited non-local outlets for home entertainment commodities (TV sets, radios, hi-fi equipment, etc.).

The classification of shopper types did not end here. Respondents were also asked to complete a psychographic instrument, indicating their agreement or disagreement with 15 opinion statements. From the information yielded by this procedure, shoppers were distinguished in more detail according to five lifestyle characteristics: fashion consciousness, self-confidence, innovativeness, financial optimism and diet-and-home.

Inshoppers were less fashion conscious than all Outshopper types. Home Entertainment Outshoppers were especially fashion conscious. Despite hypothesising that people who are prepared to explore non-local shopping centres might be expected to have greater self-confidence, the results did not consistently bear this out. Big-ticket Outshoppers and Furniture Outshoppers were actually less self-confident than Inshoppers. Outshoppers were, however, higher scorers on innovativeness, and this was especially true of Appearance Outshoppers who made more outshopping trips than any other group. Thus, Outshoppers generally desire new and different shopping experiences.

Financial optimism measured the perceived future financial success of the shoppers' household. This optimism was related to outshopping behaviour. In particular, Big-ticket, Furniture and Home Entertainment Outshoppers scored relatively high on this characteristic. Financially optimistic shoppers were more likely to search outside their local shopping area for expensive products.

The shopping expenditure profiles of Big-ticket, Furniture and Home Entertainment outshopping groups suggested strong orientations towards the diet-and-home characteristic. Home Entertainment Outshoppers were, in particular, houseproud and diet conscious. In general, outshopping took on something of a social activity for outshopper groups. Outshopper groups find outshopping a pleasant way to spend their time. This carries certain implications for strategies needed to persuade or encourage certain outshopper types to shop in local centres rather than those outside the local area. Among 'social' outshoppers a different approach is called for than among those consumers whose motivations are primarily economic. For example, improving the dining, entertainment and recreational facilities, keeping in mind the sociological and cultural backgrounds of residents, might enhance the appeal of local trade areas.

Product specific outshoppers seem to have narrow lifestyle interests that define their shopping. For example, Home Entertainment Outshoppers are very fashion conscious and self-confident. They seem to be more diet conscious and financially optimistic. Yet their socio-economic characteristics were not very different from those of Inshoppers. Local retailers of home entertainment products may therefore find it profitable to concentrate on scenarios accentuating the social interaction of fashion-oriented people in a home setting with the products as the focal point of the interaction.

FASHION

An understanding of the contemporary consumer's clothing and apparel shopping behaviour can be tremendously important for effective retail fashion marketing. Over the past few years, a growing amount of research has focused on consumer fashion behaviour, though relatively little work has been directed towards applying contemporary fashion concepts to fashion retailing (King and Ring, 1975).

Historically, much of contemporary fashion theory has focused on the characteristics of fashion innovators, opinion leaders and innovative communicators as vital links and key targets for retail sales and fashion promotional efforts. Thus, several studies (King, 1963; Darden and Reynolds, 1974; Reynolds and Darden, 1972; Summers, 1970; Baumgarten, 1975; Hirschmann and Mills, 1979) have been aimed at defining and understanding these specific market segments as they relate to fashion purchase behaviour. Another perspective has explored the link between retail store image, self-perception and store patronage (Berry, 1969; Grubb and Grathwold, 1967; Lazer and Wyckham, 1969).

Another avenue of investigation in the retail fashion area has focused on a better understanding of the fashion retailing process through the vehicle of lifestyle. This approach has been put forward by some writers as offering considerable potential in terms of identifying and profiling fashion market segments (King and Ring, 1975). Early attempts to use lifestyle measures in understanding fashion retail markets suffered from conceptual and methodological problems. Lifestyle concepts often involved general living patterns not closely related or relevant to specific retail buying situations (Wind and Green, 1974). Recent research conducted in the USA has tried to overcome these early limitations. Gutman and Mills (1982) examined overall relationships between lifestyle, self-concept, demographics, shopping orientation and fashion sense. A postal survey among approximately 6300 Los Angeles' women revealed key segments which spanned the fashion spectrum: Leaders, Followers, Independents, Neutrals, Uninvolved, Negatives and Rejectors. The analysis of these fashion segments showed their self-concepts to be meaningfully related to their fashion orientations. Demographic differences were, however, relatively unimportant as a segmentation tool. Clear and significant differences between fashion segments were revealed with respect to the store at which they reported shopping most often.

Leaders scored high on the factors of fashion leadership, interest and importance, and low on anti-fashion attitudes. Their high scores on leadership set them apart from the other segments (excepting the Independents). In accepting the 'establishment views' on fashion, they seemed to demonstrate their strong involvement with mainstream (e.g., designer fashion) looks. *Followers* exhibited a similar profile to the Leaders, but obviously had a lower score on the leadership dimension. This group would be more likely than the free-spirited Independents to emulate the leader (and it is probably true that the Leaders likewise need these Followers – it's no fun being a leader with no following). *Independents* also are fashion aware, but differ from the first two groups in their strong anti-fashion attitudes.

Independents are interested in fashion, but not in recent designers and others in the 'fashion establishment' dictating tastes for them. *Neutrals* are true to their label, with modest scores on leadership, interests and importance dimensions, showing fashion to be of only moderate significance to them. *Uninvolved* do not exhibit even a modest interest in fashion, with weak attitudes towards fashion generally. *Negatives* have no desire for leadership nor any interest in it. They do think it is moderately important to be well-dressed. But this attitude may stem more from the feeling that it is important to be 'neat and clean' than 'fashionably clothed'. Also they resent the 'fashion establishment' telling people what to wear. *Rejectors* were the mirror image of the Leaders. Their profile was similar to that of the Negatives, except that they did not attach any importance to fashion even to the point of being unconcerned with what they wear.

The Leaders and Independents saw themselves as more sophisticated, modern, different, chance taking, confident, creative and sociable and had more complicated lifestyles than other segments. The Leaders indicated that they enjoyed shopping and were not cost-conscious, practical or traditional. The Independents showed a similar pattern but scored higher on cost-consciousness. The Followers also enjoyed shopping, but scored high on traditionalism and following the fashions set by others. Relationships merged between lifestyle and fashion shopping. Leaders were young, active shoppers who thought of themselves as being modern, sophisticated, confident and very sociable in their orientation. The results suggested a significant opportunity for fashion-oriented department stores to regain some of this business (from up-market, specialty outlets) provided that adequate attention is paid to the needs of this group.

PRODUCT SPECIFIC SEGMENTATION

The first part of this chapter examined research dealing with general consumer activities in the broad sphere of retail buying behaviour. Attention is now turned to look at market segmentation research, using psychographics, in which the focus has been on consumer classifications related to single products. In this sort of research, much more information can be elicited about consumers' opinions concerning individual product categories or products. This level of analysis can reveal considerable detail about consumers' perceptions of a product and specific reasons they have for wanting to buy it or not to buy it. As will be seen, psychographic typologies have been produced for a wide range of product categories, including cars, prescription drugs, cosmetics and toiletries, foodstuffs and luxury items.

Car buying

Much of the consumer researcher's interest in personality was stimulated by Evans (1959) who attempted to test the assumption that car buyers differ in personality structure. A standard personality inventory, the Edwards Personal Preference Schedule, was administered to owners of Chevrolets and Fords. There were only a few statistically significant differences between the two groups. Using a discriminant analysis, Evans was able to predict correctly a Ford or Chevrolet owner in only 63 per cent of cases, not much better than would be expected by chance. When 12 other objectively measurable criteria of car buying were also taken into account Evans was able to predict correctly in 70 per cent of cases. He concluded therefore that personality is of relatively little value in predicting car ownership.

More recently, Young (1973) used psychographics to help position a car model – the Ford Pinto – in the United States. According to the manufacturers, the initial Pinto advertising portrayed the car as 'carefree, small (and) romantic'. The strategy was 'to sell to small car prospects; to compete against imported small cars; to say that the car was carefree, trouble free, beautifully styled and economical' (Young, 1973: 15). As the introduction of the Pinto proceeded, psychographic research disclosed that potential Pinto buyers had a less romantic orientation towards cars and driving. They endorsed statements like 'I wish I could depend on my car more', 'I am more practical in car selection', 'I like to feel how powerful my car is' and 'The only function for a car is transportation'. They rejected statements like 'The kind of car you have is important as to how people see you' and 'Taking care of a car is too much trouble'.

As a result of this research, the Pinto was repositioned (in advertising by its new agency) as 'the epitomy of function, exemplifying basic economical transportation, trading on Ford's heritage of the Model A'. Consequently, 'today Pinto is the largest selling subcompact, outselling Volkswagen by a sizeable margin' (Young, 1973: 15). It is admittedly farfetched to assume that all or maybe even most of Pinto's success was due to this change in position. But it does seem reasonable to believe that emphasis on economy and practicality appealed to the salient needs of potential buyers, and that the revised message communicated ideas that potential customers would find most persuasive.

Prescription drugs

Ziff (1971) surveyed 2000 housewives across the USA. They were given 214 attitude statements; their responses to these statements were factor analysed to produce a general classification of the group as a whole. In addition, separate analyses were computed on selections of items dealing with specific product categories: drugs, personal and household items. She reports the classification for drug use only – among the product classifications. There were four categories derived: (i) Realists; (ii) Authority Seekers; (iii) Sceptics; and (iv) Hypochondriacs.

Realists are not health fatalists, nor excessively concerned with protection or germs. They view remedies positively, want something that is convenient and works, and do not feel the need for a doctor-recommended medicine. *Authority Seekers* are doctor and prescription oriented; are neither fatalists nor stoics concerning health, but they prefer the stamp of authority on what they do take. *Sceptics* have a low health concern, and are least likely to resort to medication and are highly sceptical of cold remedies. *Hypochondriacs* have high health concern, regard themselves as prone to any bug going around and tend to take medication at the first symptom. They do not look for strength in what they take, but need some mild authority reassurance.

In examining relationships between product usage and segmentation solely derived from drug-related statements, Ziff found some interesting results. As expected Hypochondriacs were high in usage, the Sceptics were low, and the Realists and Authority Seekers in between. Attitudes related to a product category can provide insights into product related values which offer guidance that is of direct use and relevance to advertising and marketing approaches for the target market segment.

Stomach remedy

Pernica (1974) reported on a market segmentation study of consumers of a stomach remedy. He developed a list of 80 items that included symptom frequency and benefits provided by different brands, attitudes towards treatment and beliefs about ailments. Items tapping general personality traits were recast so as to be product specific. For instance, 'I worry too much' was translated into 'I seem to get stomach problems if I worry too much'. The 80 product-specific items were reduced to 13 factors and scores on the latter were obtained for each respondent. The resultant consumer segments

(Severe Sufferers, Active Medicators, Hypochondriacs and Practicalists) were described in terms of personality traits, lifestyle attributes and demographic information about respondents. The outcome of this research was consistent with other studies. When segmentation is based upon the dimensions on which other brands differ, they were much more readily discriminating than when it was based on more general considerations.

The Severe Sufferers are the extreme group on the potency side of the market. They tend to be young, have children and be well educated. They are irritable and anxious people and believe that they suffer more severely than others. They take the ailments seriously, fuss about it, pamper themselves and keep trying new and different products.

The Active Medicators are on the same side of the motivational spectrum. They are typically modern suburbanites with average income and education. They are emotionally adjusted to the demands of their active lives. They use remedies to relieve every ache and pain.

The Hypochondriacs are on the opposite side of the motivational spectrum. They tend to be older, not as well educated and female. They have conservative attitudes towards medication and a deep concern over health. They see possible dangers in the frequent use of remedies, are concerned over side effects and are afraid of remedies with new ingredients and extra potency. They are strongly oriented toward medical authority, seeking guidance in treatment.

The Practicalists are in the extreme position on this side of the motivational spectrum. They tend to be older, well educated, emotionally the most stable and the least concerned over their ailment or the dangers of remedies. They accept the ailment and its discomforts as a part of life, without fuss and pampering. They use a remedy as a last resort.

Men's toiletries

Furse and Greenberg (1975) produced a two-fold segmentation in examining men's attitudes towards toiletries. The two segments were labelled 'Mr Practical' and 'The Fun-Loving Routine-User'. Two lesser types were isolated – a type concerned with aftershave as an adjunct to sexual role-playing and a conservative non-user type – but both categorised considerably fewer respondents than the first two.

Mr Practical was found to be oriented towards practicality. Although a user of aftershave, this type of user generally rejected packaging and advertising influences on brand choice. He disdained

promotional images, but agreed with the physical se
cleanliness and freshness, associated with such produ
to being pragmatic, Mr Practical was also conformist
about purchase and use of the product, as demonstra
ment with statements such as 'Women introduce men to
buying them as gifts' and 'Men tend to use the same   as
someone else whose opinion they respect'.

The Fun-Loving Routine-User did not consider the use of aftershave and cologne as serious behaviour, but merely a bit of good fun.
This segment favoured the use of aftershave because it was seen as a
product that is personally pleasant and because it makes a person
smell better and, perhaps, more pleasant to be around in social
situations. This type of person rejected ideas associated with psychological reasons for use of the product, such as 'Shaving gives a man
self-awareness' and 'Aftershave is a sign of masculinity'. However,
this person enjoyed the consumption of promotional and advertising
images which did not take themselves too seriously. The Fun-Loving
Routine-User did not view aftershave as something that is strongly
related to sexual behaviour, but did agree that men like to feel attractive to women, and cologne reinforces this feeling. In general this
type tended to be a routine user of this product and was likely to try a
variety of brands.

Male attitudes were found to be related to responses to advertising,
specifically for toiletry advertising, but they were not related either to
product usage or brand loyalty among this sample. Furse and Greenberg suggest, however, that this result might be due in part to artificial
features of the study which used a sample entirely composed of
college students and the fact that only two major attitudinal segments
were employed as discriminating variables.

The same study also investigated the feasibility of using cognitive
style as a market segmentation variable. Cognitive style represents a
set of predispositions influencing an individual's information
gathering and processing behaviour. Taken together these cognitive
style characteristics are presumed to represent relatively stable strategies which regulate how an individual processes his or her everyday
experiences. Furse and Greenberg found that their sample was
characterised by such cognitive style attributes as an orientation
towards processing information through the written word, or through
the spoken word or via pictures. Some respondents had relatively
strong orientations towards smell, touch and other kinds of sensory
input. Cognitive style tended not to be strongly related to product
usage or brand preference, but was linked to mass media consumption.

example, respondents with orientations towards the written word exhibited strong preferences for print media, particularly for magazines; while those with an orientation towards the spoken word preferred television. Cognitive style was seen as having potential to guide decision making in the sphere of new product promotion. Knowing about consumers' preferred strategies for processing information could not only help decide upon media placement of promotions, but also in respect of the design of the promotional messages themselves.

Pet food

A further example of a product-specific lifestyle study is an extensive marketing research exercise carried out in the United States by General Foods in 1970. General Foods performed this psychographic study to determine which types of consumers were most likely to buy dog food, and, in turn, what kind of dog food would be most appealing to them.

The results indicated that there were six distinct types of dog owners. Two of the six segments were judged to be the best market targets for the proposed new product. Consumers in one of these target segments tended to regard their dogs as 'baby substitutes'. This segment was made up mostly of women who did not have children and who lived in small apartments in the city. The women were willing to spend a lot of money on dog food, allowed their dogs to be finicky eaters and often tended to switch brands.

The other market segment consumers were described as 'the nutritionalists'. The consumers were profiled as intelligent dog owners, well educated and possessing high incomes. Many people in this group were willing to spend a lot of money to keep their dogs healthy.

Cameras

Hughes (1978) attempted an interesting analysis of the camera market by looking at how three groups were rated: all camera purchasers, those who bought more expensive cameras and those who specifically bought Nikon cameras. As Table 6.1 shows, the camera purchasers were asked to rate themselves against a series of characteristics and these various characteristics discriminate between the different groups. Thus, compared to purchasers of more expensive cameras, Nikon camera purchasers tended to see themselves as more broad-minded, discriminating, efficient and intelligent, but less reserved, conformist and persuadable.

Table 6.1 Psychographic profiles of camera purchasers (index: all adults = 100)

	All camera purchasers	More expensive cameras	Nikon cameras
Awkward	106	79	77
Broad-minded	112	123	150
Creative	119	141	158
Dominating	120	137	154
Efficient	114	130	150
Intelligent	117	156	206
Refined	110	127	136
Reserved	100	103	71
Stubborn	114	107	93
Tense	103	100	84
Conformist	88	93	59
Economy-minded	100	96	77
Experimenter	96	91	74
Persuasible	104	93	47
Style-conscious	114	92	67

Note: These data were derived from self-ratings on groups of adjectives (e.g. dominating: authoritarian, demanding, aggressive) or phrases (e.g. conformist: 'I prefer to buy things my friends would approve of'). The ratings were on a five point scale from 'agree a lot' to 'disagree a lot'.
Source: Target Group Index; quoted in G.D. Hughes (1978) *Marketing Management*, Reading, Mass.; Addison-Wesley. Reproduced by permission of the author.

Purchasing lottery tickets

A psychographic profiling analysis of state lottery ticket purchasers in the United States was carried out by McConkey and Warren (1987). Comparisons were made between heavy, light and non-purchasers of lottery tickets among nearly 4000 female members of a consumer panel residing in 16 lottery states. An extensive self-completion questionnaire was mailed to panel members, of whom some 42 per cent replied. Among the items on the questionnaire were 200 psychographic statements derived from a number of earlier psychographic studies. These responses were grouped through statistical analysis into 38 factors on which lottery ticket purchasers and non-purchasers were compared.

Distinct psychological character profiles emerged for consumer groups defined by the level of ticket purchase. Heavier purchasers were more likely to be over-eaters and to prefer urban living than the

Table 6.2   Benefit segments in the less expensive camera market

---

The 'Do-It-Yourselfer' (25 per cent)
Great pride in good pictures
Gratification from making settings and adjustments
Pride in a complex camera
Regards a good picture the result of his expertise

The 'Black Box User' (40 per cent)
Taking pictures considered a necessary evil
Little pride expressed if the picture is good
Desire for camera to be as simple as possible

The 'Timid Photographer' (35 per cent)
Great pride in good pictures
High perceived risk that pictures will not be good
No confidence in ability to manipulate camera and settings
Desires camera to guarantee good pictures without his effort

Source: J.F. Engel, H.F. Fiorello and M.A. Cayley (eds) (1972) *Market Segmentation*,
New York: Holt, Rinehart and Winston, p.18. Reproduced by permission of the
publisher.

other two groups. They appeared to be somewhat tense and less
health conscious, perhaps reflecting the fast urban pace and heavy
pressure placed on young working mothers. However, they were
surprisingly less mobile, based on their desire to live in the same town
for life and their lack of desire to travel outside the United States
compared to non-purchasers of lottery tickets.

Non-purchasers of lottery tickets were less optimistic and had
conservative views towards excessive use of 'sex' on television and in
commercials. They reflected the traditional roles of women in society
as homemakers who viewed the man as the boss in the home and
believed that men are smarter than women. They were more health
conscious, being the least likely to over-eat, consume snack foods or
routinely consume some alcoholic beverages.

The characteristics of the light purchasers of lottery tickets generally fell in between those of non-purchasers and heavy purchasers.
However, there were some exceptions. Lighter purchasers rated
highest in the following categories: optimism, conscientious consumers, child orientation, kitchen orientation and uptightness. They
rated lowest of the three groups in traditionality, foreign travel and
buy American orientation. It appeared that they might try to be
involved in everything, and this approach of spreading themselves so
thin was reflected in their being more uptight (tense) than those in the
other two groups.

CONCLUSION

Psychographic segmentation of consumer activities and products can provide important insights into the nature of markets. Psychographic profiles can offer a much richer description of potential or actual marks for products than demographics alone. This information can assist marketers to make decisions in attempting to match a product's image with the type of consumer most likely to purchase (and to re-purchase). As an example, consider the profiles of heavy users of eye make-up and shortening (see Table 6.3) as described by Wells and Beard (1974).

While it is clear that heavy and light users of eye make-up and shortening differed in terms of their demographic characteristics, 'other' product use and media preferences – all of which provide valuable marketing information – and their respective psychographic profiles reveal a great deal more about each market segment. The psychological portraits of these two sets of consumers provide insights into what makes them tick, and the kinds of marketing messages each is likely to be most responsive to. The value of psychographics lies not simply in its provision of additional dimensions along which to classify consumers, but more especially because those dimensions have a dynamic quality. They are not just outwardly descriptive, but more significantly inwardly revealing, and represent operational indications of internal forces which motivate consumers.

Table 6.3 Profile of heavy users of eye make-up and shortening

	Heavy user of eye make-up	Heavy user of shortening
Demographic characteristics	Young, well educated, lives in metropolitan areas.	Middle-aged, medium to large family lives outside metropolitan area.
Product use	Also a heavy user of liquid face make-up, lipstick, hair spray, perfume, cigarettes, gasoline.	Also a heavy user of flour, sugar, canned lunch meat, cooked pudding, catsup.
Media preferences	Fashion magazines, 'The Tonight Show', adventure programmes.	Reader's Digest, daytime TV serials, family-situation TV comedies.
Activities, interests and opinions		
Agrees more than average with:	'I often try the latest hairdo styles when they change' 'An important part of my life and activities is dressing smartly' 'I like to feel attractive to men' 'I want to look a little different from others' 'I like what I see when I look in the mirror' 'I take good care of my skin' 'I would like to spend a year in London or Paris' 'I like ballet' 'I like to serve unusual dinners' 'I really do believe that blondes have more fun'	'I love to bake and frequently do' 'I save recipes from newspapers and magazines' 'I love to eat' 'I enjoy most forms of housework' 'Usually I have regular days for washing, cleaning, etc. around the house' 'I am uncomfortable when my house is not completely clean' 'I try to arrange my home for my children's convenience' 'Our family is a close knit group' 'Clothes should be dried in the fresh air and out-of-doors' 'I would rather spend a quiet evening at home than go out to a party'

Disagrees more than average with:

'I enjoy most forms of housework'
'I furnish my home for comfort, not for style'
'If it was good enough for my mother, it's good enough for me'

'My idea of housekeeping is once over lightly'
'Classical music is more interesting than popular music'
'I like ballet'
'I'd like to spend a year in London or Paris'

Source: Wells and Beard (1974) 'Personality and consumer behaviour', in S. Ward and T.S. Robertson (eds.), *Consumer Behaviour: Theoretical Sources*, Englewood Cliffs, NJ: Prentice Hall. Reproduced by permission of the publisher.

7 Applications of psychographics: II. Media markets

INTRODUCTION

The psychographic segmentation of media markets is bound up with conceptual arguments about the activity or passivity of media consumers. This argument addresses the issue of how consumers use the media. Are consumers generally active in their relations with mass media? Or do they usually allow the media to wash over them? Although it highlights an important conceptual distinction, this dichotomy of media use is itself an oversimplification. In practice, media consumers are most likely to exhibit both active and passive characteristics. Much more important is to identify the styles of media use that may be exhibited by the same individuals on different occasions and in connection with different media or types of media content.

Before turning to psychographic studies of media markets, it is worth making mention of several areas of communication research that have generated audience classification while investigating the issue of the 'active' audience. Audiences can display activity in various ways. Among the more significant of these are selectivity, utility, intentionality and involvement.

The notion of selectivity refers to activity in making a choice about using media. A number of different types of decisions may be important here. To begin with, a media consumer must make a decision to use a particular medium. Thus, a person may decide to watch television in preference to listening to the radio or reading a book. The decision process may not end simply with the selection of television. The individual may continue to watch only if there is something on that he or she wants or likes to see. Selectivity thus embodies decisions about specific media content as well as about media channels. While watching, the viewer may furthermore pay selective attention to certain aspects of a programme.

There is some evidence that selective exposure to mass communications may be determined by the need to obtain particular kinds of information (Mendelsohn, 1983), to have certain beliefs reinforced (Gunter and Wober, 1983) or to bring about changes in unpleasant mood states (Boyanowsky, 1977; Zillmann and Bryant, 1985). Meanwhile, selective perception and memory of programme content may be produced by pre-existing beliefs and stereotypes.

Activity can be defined in terms of the utility of the media by consumers. Individuals can be selective not simply in their choice of media, but also in so far as media content is selectively chosen for the purpose of satisfying particular needs and motives (Katz, Blumler and Gurevitch, 1974; Palmgreen and Rayburn, 1982; Rubin, 1981, 1983). Within the uses and gratifications perspective, different investigators have identified long lists of reasons people give for using media.

Some researchers have found that different clusters of claimed gratifications obtained – for example, from television – are related in different ways to different preferred areas of programming (Rubin, 1979). Although this type of audience activity analysis can be useful, it is not without its problems both conceptually and methodologically. The endorsement of simple statements that express reasons for media use, for instance, probably only scratches the surface and does not provide a proper measure of the underlying psychological antecedents of selective exposure to media. Another point is that gratification statements often tend to make reference only to the medium as a whole. In other words, 'I watch TV to learn about the world', 'I watch TV to relax' and so on refer to reasons for watching television *per se.* But television schedules contain a wide variety of different kinds of programmes. Each of these gratifications may apply as reasons for watching a number of programme types, while with regard to other types they may not be relevant. Researchers' attempts to get at 'activity' in television viewing have often, therefore, failed to probe deeply enough to give a proper idea of the nature and degree of that activity across different viewing fare.

Another sense in which audience activity has generated distinctions is in respect of the intentionality of media use. In other words, to what extent is media use driven by prior motives and needs. These motives may stem from personality characteristics of individuals. Individuals may, for example, be driven to watch programmes which reinforce certain values and beliefs. There is also evidence that individuals with particular attitudinal or behavioural dispositions may in the longer term tend to move towards certain types of media content. Individuals of an aggressive nature, for instance, have been found to exhibit preferences for violent media content (Atkin, Greenberg, Korzenny and McDermott, 1979; Gunter, 1985).

Finally, there is the idea of audience activity as involvement. Involvement can occur at any of several distinct levels – cognitive, affective and behavioural. Cognitive effort may be invested in following a storyline when watching a televised drama, taking in information from television news broadcasts and in making judgements about the content of programmes (e.g., whether to believe what is shown). Effectively, the extent to which audiences get involved with television programmes may depend on how much viewers identify with television characters and empathise with or 'feel for' them in the predicaments in which they are portrayed. Audience involvement with television drama characters and other personalities on the screen may manifest itself behaviourally in parasocial interaction. Both young viewers (Greenberg, 1976) and older viewers (Rubin and Rubin, 1982) have indicated companionship as an important function of television. Typologies of viewers can be derived in terms of their involvement with television programmes in this sense.

SEGMENTING MEDIA MARKETS

The media industry is experiencing rapid, unprecedented growth. The numbers of television channels, radio stations and newspapers and magazines, both generalised and specialised in content, are increasing all the time. In this ever more competitive environment, it is becoming important for media producers and distributors to understand how best to satisfy their consumers' needs.

Conceptual framework

Two basic approaches to examining differences in media market characteristics have been identified in earlier writings on the subject (e.g., Tigert, 1974). One approach is to examine the characteristics of a particular medium's market and to examine those characteristics with the characteristics of those who are not in the medium's market. In other words, one can compare viewers with non-viewers for particular television channels or types of programming, or readers with non-readers for particular newspapers and magazines, and so on. The merit of this approach lies in the fact that the researcher is examining mutually exclusive groups. In principle, this should provide an opportunity for large differences to occur between market segments.

A problem with this approach is that in today's multi-media environment with increasing numbers of newspapers and magazines, radio stations and television channels, identifying individuals who may never have experienced a particular media outlet may be difficult. Although with television, for example, just a few channels may occupy the greatest slice of the viewing cake, there may be considerable overlap between their respective audiences, and the same may be true even of minor channels which achieve only small audience shares. Viewers tend to explore whatever is available and may watch just a few channels for most of the time, but from time-to-time also dip into many other available channels.

A second approach involves the examination of a particular medium's market characteristics in relation to the characteristics of market members for other media. A comparison across markets may reveal interesting information about differences in the 'quality' of the market. This may be especially important for advertising or promotional campaigns interested in reaching particular population subgroups, while at the same time needing to be as economical as possible in the volume of expenditure. Thus, it may be more efficient to discover where the target group can be found in the greatest concentration through careful selection of media outlets, rather than simply to hope to reach them through a mass targeting campaign.

Problems can occur with this approach, however, when strong overlaps exist between audiences for different media outlets. Under these circumstances, it could be difficult to uncover significant psychographic differences between media markets whose respective membership contain many of the same people. There are several ways around this dilemma. One solution is to remove the common market (e.g., audience) element for a pair of media outlets under examination and then to profile the non-overlap portions of the two markets. Another approach is to first of all cluster media into homogeneous 'types' through a statistical technique called factor analysis or some other appropriate technique. Having segmented the relevant media into general categories, it will then be possible to examine the characteristics of the markets (audiences) of each of the media groups, either by comparing across groups or by examining the specific characteristics of the audience of a particular media group (i.e., viewers versus non-viewers).

If psychographic research is to be useful in segmenting media markets, it must demonstrate an ability to identify unique market characteristics for individual media or media types. Furthermore, the identification of unique market characteristics must aid in the selection of appropriate media for specific products or in the development of better advertising copy for specific media.

The first major studies relating psychographic measures to media exposure were reported by Bass, Pessemeier and Tigert (1969). Wilson reported on the relationship between homemaker living patterns, product consumption and magazine readership. He concluded that living patterns (his term for lifestyle) could account for up to 30 per cent of the variance in product consumption and for up to 20–25 per cent of the variance in readership levels. Wilson introduced such lifestyle concepts as 'the happy housekeeper', 'the special shopper', 'fashion consciousness', 'the venturesome shopper', 'the weight watcher', 'beauty conscious', and so on.

Building on this work, Bass, Pessemeier and Tigert (1969) clustered respondents into readership groups and successfully discriminated among the groups using lifestyle characteristics, demographic variables, product usage variables and occupation choice characteristics. These same variable sets were then used in a simulated media selection mode to demonstrate their usefulness in media selection strategy.

TELEVISION AUDIENCE SEGMENTATION

Television is the most powerful mass medium. For a long time, while there were few channels, broadcasters enjoyed a near monopoly situation in which they were guaranteed large audiences. All this is now changing. With the expansion of services and the creation of multi-channel media environments, the audience is fragmenting and individual services have to compete more fiercely than heretofore for viewers. Television programming gratifies certain needs of the viewer by functioning as a form of entertainment, information and edification. To understand the relationship between television and its viewers, it is necessary to know what audience members expect of television and why they are motivated to watch – what needs television programming fulfils and what satisfaction it brings.

Considered in this context, programming is no different from products. Neither has 'mass appeal' in the sense that undifferentiated marketing of them is efficient. The segmentation of audiences is as logical as the segmentation of markets. Yet purely demographic segmentation makes no more sense for television audiences than it does for product markets. There is a distinct limit to how well traditional ratings data can portray programme audiences.

The potential viewing population is not composed of a mass of individuals homogenous in their needs and interests, but rather of definable segments of individuals, each with its own different patterns of interest they wish to address and seeking satisfaction of different psychological needs.

There is a growing realisation that a significant determinant of programme selection is to be found in viewers' expectation of television. What and how one watches depends on what one hopes to gain from the experience.

Developing audience types

The bulk of empirical research in this general area has been devoted to deriving programme categories or viewer groups on the basis of patterns of viewing (e.g., Bowman and Farley, 1972; Ehrenberg, 1968; Frost, 1969; Goodhart, Ehrenberg and Collins, 1975; Kirsch and Banks, 1962; Tigert, 1971; Watt and Krull, 1974; Wells, 1969).

Need-based typologies

The exception is found in the stream of research that has come to be called 'need gratification' (Bower, 1973; Frank and Greenberg, 1980; Glick and Levy, 1962; Greenberg, Dervin and Dominick, 1968; Katz, Blumler and Gurevitch, 1974; Rubin, 1981; Steiner, 1963) which proposes that watching television fulfils certain needs of viewers and that these, in large measure, explain why (and what programmes) they watch.

The recognition of the audience as active rather than passive in its selection of programmes in order to satisfy certain interests or needs, led Frank and Greenberg (1980, 1984) to explore what these needs are and how they relate to patterns of programme preference and viewing. They found that audience segments defined in terms of viewers' interests and needs may or may not correspond to the traditional demographic categories predominantly used by the television industry.

Frank and Greenberg investigated the leisure interests and activities of individuals, the needs satisfied by the latter, television viewing behaviour and reactions to television programmes. Instruments were developed through desk research and qualitative pilot surveys, before being distributed to a large, representative survey sample. Through a series of factor and cluster analyses, the authors derived 14 interest segments. These are shown in Tables 7.1 and 7.2,

Table 7.1 Interest factor summary

---

1. *Comprehensive news and information*: economy, unemployment, taxes, legal process in courts, morality in politics, sources and uses of energy, social security, preventative medicine, labour unions, welfare.

2. *Athletic activities*: (participant) snow skiing, water skiing, tennis, volleyball, squash.

3. *Household activities*: cleaning, meal preparation, sewing, needlework, household management.

4. *Classical arts*: opera, classical music, ballet, live theatre, literature.

5. *Reaping nature's benefits*: fishing, hunting, agriculture and farming, gardening.

6. *Professional sports*: baseball, basketball, football, boxing, golf.

7. *Science and engineering*: chemistry, electronics, medical sciences, engineering, geology.

8. *Popular entertainment*: visiting friends, radio, travel/sightseeing, popular music (jazz, folk, rock, country, etc.), dining out, cinema, driving/motoring, television, entertainment at home.

9. *Religion*: religious organisation activities, religion.

10. *Popular social issues*: sex education, sex attitudes, rights of minorities, occult, women's rights.

11. *Indoor games*: board games, crossword/jigsaw puzzles, chess/checkers, playing cards.

12. *Community activities*: community social functions, charities and civic associations, local cultural activities.

13. *Investments*: real estate, managing a business, stock market.

14. *International affairs*: arms race, balance of trade, conflict in Middle East.

15. *Camping out*: camping, backpacking, boating, hiking.

16. *Crime and society*: capital punishment, abortion, causes and prevention of crime.

17. *Mechanical activities*: auto repair and racing, model building, engineering, electronics, motorcycles.

18. *Contemporary dancing*: modern dance, dancing (discotheque, ballroom, etc.).

Source: Frank and Greenberg (1984). Reproduced by permission of the publisher.

and are further elaborated in Figure 7.3. They were based on reported leisure interests and activities. Next, the needs satisfied by these interests were scaled down to nine basic types of need (see Table 7.3).

Table 7.2 Overview of 14 interest segments

	Percentage of sample (average)	Average age (years)	Females in segment (%) (average)	Females in sample (%)
Adult male concentration				
Mechanics and outdoor life	7	29	4	1
Money and nature's products	7	53	23	3
Family and community centred	8	47	17	2
Female concentration				
Elderly concerns	7	61	71	11
Arts and cultural activities	7	44	69	11
Home and community centred	8	44	84	12
Family-integrated activities	8	35	87	16
Youth concentration				
Competitive sports	8	22	5	1
Science/engineering				
Athletic and social activities	5	19	83	7
Indoor games and social activities	6	22	91	7
Mixed				
News and information	6	47	43	4
Detached	9	46	47	8
Cosmopolitan self-enrichment	5	36	59	9
Highly diversified	9	34	51	8
Total	100	40	52	100

Source: Frank and Greenberg (1984). Reproduced by permission of the publisher.

Table 7.1 contains a 'thumbnail' sketch of the television viewing behaviour of each of the 18 interest segments. From these profiles it can be seen that programmes and programme types are related in an interpretable and meaningful fashion to the interests, needs and demographic characteristics of viewers. Table 7.2 indicates how the interest segments are distributed across the population and Table 7.3 provides further profiles of need types.

Frank and Greenberg (1984) provided examples of the ways in which their interest-based segments of the audience were related to television viewing patterns and preferences. Focusing on the Adult Female Concentration segment, which in turn was subdivided into four categories, they showed that not only did each of these sub-categories have distinctive patterns of interests but were also distinguishable in terms of the programmes they most liked to watch.

Table 7.3 Need factor summary

---

1. *Socially stimulating*: to find my ideas are often shared by others, to be interesting and stimulating to other people about things I'm familiar with, to feel good about life in general, to meet new people.

2. *Status enhancement*: to impress people, to feel more important than I am, to have more influence on other people, to be like other people, to compete against others.

3. *Unique/creative accomplishment*: to really excel in my life, to be more of a leader, to feel unique/different, to compete against others, to feel creative.

4. *Escape from problems*: to get away from pressures and responsibilities of home/work, to relax, to forget about my problems, to escape from reality.

5. *Family ties*: to feel closer to my family, to spend time with my family, to develop strong family ties.

6. *Understanding others*: to understand how people think, to better understand people's behaviour, to get the most out of life's daily experiences, to know that others' problems are the same as mine.

7. *Greater self-acceptance*: to lift my spirits, to understand myself better, to overcome loneliness, to feel I am using my time in the best way.

8. *Escape from boredom*: to be entertained, to kill time, to escape from reality.

9. *Intellectual stimulation and growth*: to find out how things work, to learn new thoughts and ideas, to learn about new things to do and places to see, to learn about what is going on in the world.

Source: Frank and Greenberg (1984). Reproduced by permission of the publisher.

The Elderly Concerns category, for example, were especially likely to watch variety shows, general dramas and game shows. The Arts and Cultural Activities segment had the highest liking for theatrical performances and musical performances on television of any sub-category. The Home and Community Centred type did not exhibit any outstanding television preferences compared with other groups, and the Family-Integrated Activities group, while heavier viewers generally than the former, also did not show a strongly idiosyncratic television viewing profile. Their most liked programmes were situation comedy and crime dramas. Frank and Greenberg hypothesised, however, that the Family-Integrated Activites group tended to be more influenced by children and teenagers in what they watched than any other audience group. This conclusion was not simply derived from the fact that these people contained a high proportion of households with children and teenagers in residence, but more importantly from the finding that children and teenagers made such an impact on the stated needs, interests and viewing behaviour of adults in this segment.

A different need-based typology has been produced by Domzal and Kernan (1983) who were inspired by an earlier conceptual model proposed by Glick and Levy (1962). The latter suggested that there are essentially only three kinds of television viewer:

(1) those who embrace the medium, accepting it with considerable enjoyment and use;
(2) those who protest against it, feeling and/or expressing concern over what it 'does to them'; and
(3) those who accommodate television, balancing its desirable and undesirable features.

Domzal and Kernan (1983) conducted further research from the need-gratification perspective to assess relationships between audience segments and programme preferences. This study investigated patterns of programming choice among different audience segments, differences in programme perceptions and evaluation, and other media usage habits and preferences that characterise television audience segments. They had respondents evaluate programme excerpts and give their opinions on a long list of AIO statements derived from a number of sources and dealing with different lifestyle issues. Information was also obtained on demographic factors and other media habits.

Domzal and Kernan's results neatly conformed with Glick and Levy's three-fold classification. Their first segment appeared to be a group of Television Embracers and included people who were apparently willing to watch most types of programmes and did so on an occasional or regular basis. These Embracers watched mainly to escape from their problems and to relax. They found television a pleasant way to spend an evening, watched more 'escapist' types of programmes and did most of their viewing from habit. Although they did not believe that television is perfect in every way, most were generally satisfied with its programming. This group of viewers took on an 'emotion' orientation from Frank and Greenberg's (1980) need-satisfaction paradigm – that is, viewing for relaxation or for forgetting problems, for being entertained, or for feeling something in common with other people. Embracers' psychographic profile reflected their interests in being entertained. Among the activities that most interested them were basketball, baseball, dancing, listening to the radio and watching television.

Television Embracers were the heaviest listeners of radio, and read mostly local news, gardening, travel, cooking, entertainment, sports and comics in the newspaper. They were the lightest readers of books and read mostly mysteries. In movies, they preferred love and romance, horror and disaster films, and were the heaviest readers of fashion magazines and women's magazines.

Television Accommodators had choice patterns similar to embracers but tended to prefer programmes with serious content, whether news, drama or comedy. Accommodators were most interested in activities such as backpacking, ballet, cycling, community social functions, gourmet cooking, hiking, local cultural activities, movies, opera and sculpture. They were also interested in conservation and ecology issues, consumerism and rights of minority groups. Accommodators' newspaper reading centred on world and national news, and the business and property sections. They also read mostly mysteries, historical novels, psychology and self-help books. Accommodators were the heaviest movie goers, and their favourites included comedies, science fiction, musicals and crime/spy thrillers.

Television Protesters represented the most selective group in choosing television programming. They watched selected news and high-brow dramas and comedies on a regular basis. Protesters described television as 'in bad taste', 'dull', 'all the same' and 'simple minded'. Their viewing centred around learning something and knowing what is going on in the world. From the need-satisfaction perspective, protesters had a strong 'knowledge orientation' towards television. They felt that watching television was worthwhile so long as they learned something from it. Their psychographic profile revealed activities such as classical music, literature, live theatre, paintings and visiting friends to be of most interest. They were also interested in such issues as the arms race, balance of trade, conflict in the Middle East, national economy and women's rights and roles. The protesters were the lightest radio listeners, and then listened mostly to classical, popular and instrumental programmes. Newspaper readership centred around the editorial pages and their favourite books were fiction and 'how-to' books. They were generally in the highest income bracket of all groups.

PSYCHOGRAPHIC AUDIENCE TYPOLOGIES

While numerous studies have revealed differences in media preferences, evaluations and actual consumption patterns in relation to age, sex and social class dimensions, a handful of studies have attempted to classify audiences along psychological dimensions (Furse and Greenberg, 1975; Teel, Bearden and Durand, 1979). These audience segmentation studies are of particular interest to advertisers who want to select media outlets likely to deliver the largest audience of potential customers. In addition, Gensch and Ranganathan (1974) demonstrated that programme preferences provided separate and useful information about the female consumer of selected products. Regular purchasers of lipstick appeared to have a bias towards movies and westerns, independently of what would be indicated by their demographics.

Research by Peterson (1972) revealed distinct consumer types with respect to general media exposure patterns (i.e. newspaper, magazines, television and radio). These types were discernible with respect to individual psychological and demographic configurations. In this age, however, demographic variables were better discriminators of media consumption patterns than were personality variables as measured by the Edwards Personality Preference Schedule. It has already been noted that most clinically derived personality scales often generalise only poorly to the consumer context. More recent work using specially developed variables can be powerful predictors of media exposure and behaviours.

Teel, Bearden and Durand (1979) conducted research in an attempt to characterise audiences of radio and television in psychographic terms. A random sample of over 750 individuals from a south-western city of the USA were interviewed face-to-face and information obtained from them on their demographic characteristics, media behaviours and psychographic attributes, operationalised in terms of 29 activity, interest and opinion (AIO) statements. Statistical factoring yielded five psychographic types. These types together with sample AIO statements are reproduced from Teel:

A. Old-Fashioned Factor
    Sample statement: 'I have some old-fashioned tastes and habits'.
B. Outgoing/Individualist Factor
    Sample statement: 'I'd rather try to fix something myself before taking it to an expert'.
C. Service/Quality-Conscious Factor
    Sample statement: 'Banking is so important to me that I would go out of my way to find a bank with good personal service'.
D. Fashion-Conscious Factor
    Sample statement: 'If my clothes aren't in fashion, it really bothers me'.
E. Other-Directed Factor
    Sample statement: 'I usually ask for help from other people in deciding what to do'.

On relating these psychographic characteristics to radio and television usage, Teel *et al.* found that television viewers differed from non-viewers and radio listeners from non-listeners in a number of systematic ways. Averaged over the day, television viewers seemed more outgoing and individualistic in their behaviour than non-viewers and concerned themselves more with service support in the marketplace. Unique psychographic audience profiles contributed to this composite picture of the television audience within day-parts. For example, members of the daytime television audience were more old-fashioned and less other-directed than non-members. In fact, daytime television viewers were significantly more old-fashioned than both daytime radio listeners and late-night television viewers. Viewers who stayed up late to watch television were less old-fashioned, more outgoing and individualistic, more concerned with service quality considerations and more fashion conscious than non-late-night television viewers. They were significantly less old-fashioned than any other television daytime audience, but did not differ a great deal from the night radio audience. Daytime radio listeners were less old-fashioned, more outgoing and individualistic, and more fashion conscious than non-listeners.

As with television, this summary profile concealed unique psychographic characteristics of the different radio daytime audiences. For instance, people who listened to radio in the morning or driving to work differed from non-listeners at this time on outgoing individualism and fashion consciousness, while members of the daytime audience were more fashion conscious than individuals who did not listen to daytime radio. Members of the radio audience in the late afternoon differed from non-members in terms of being less old-fashioned, more likely to be outgoing and individualistic, more fashion conscious and more other-directed.

The researchers concluded that radio and television audiences can be meaningfully and usefully segmented in psychographic terms. Information about psychographic segments as such can be especially useful to advertisers and marketers who want to know how best to target their commercials and promotions to reach those population sub-groups interested in their products and services.

HOME VIDEO

Potter, Forrest, Sapolsky and Ware (1988) conducted a study to explore the segmentation of VCR owners. Previous research had dealt with VCR users as one undifferentiated mass. Potter *et al.* wished to demonstrate that the VCR has reached a level of penetration where users should no longer be regarded as a single, homogenous group. Rather there is a variety of different types of people who own VCRs, and these individuals have very different patterns of usage.

Potter *et al.* obtained psychographic measures via two instruments. First, they assessed respondents' general values as delineated by the terminal and instrumental value inventory of Rokeach (1973). The second consisted of a battery of 19 activity, interest and opinion statements (AIOs) to which the respondents selected a reaction along a five-point agree–disagree scale.

Respondents were categorised as belonging to one of five segments: *Time Shifter, Source Shifter, Videophile, Low User* and *Regular User*, on the basis of their claims about VCR usage. Respondents were assigned to membership of one of these five segments by using the following procedure. First, two indices were created. The time-shifting index is the sum of responses to the items 'How often do you record programmes while watching TV?' and 'How often do you record programmes while using a timer?' The source-shifting index was the sum of responses to the following two questions: 'How often do you view rented pre-recorded tapes?' and 'How often do you view purchased pre-recorded tapes?' Respondents were then arrayed on each index according to their scores. The arrays were then divided into three categories: heavy use, medium use and light or no use. Time Shifters were those respondents who were high (at least one standard deviation above the mean) on the time-shifting index. Source Shifters were those people who were high on the source shifting index and low on the time shifting index. Respondents who were high on both indices were labelled as Videophiles. People who were low on both indices were regarded as Low Users. The remaining subjects were categorised as Regular Users.

As a validation check, the variables used to segment the respondents were examined to determine whether their means differed across groups. Significant differences were found among the VCR owner groups on all five segmenting variables. Videophiles were found to record the highest number of programmes with viewing per month at 7.8, while Source Shifters and Low Users recorded very little at 1.3 and 1.6 programmes per month, respectively. The Time Shifters used their timers most frequently at 9.5 times per month, while the Source Shifters (1.2 times) and Low Users (1.7) rarely used their timers to record programmes. Also, as expected, the two groups who played back their self-recorded tapes most frequently were the Time Shifters (9.7) and the Videophiles (9.3). As for the viewing of rented tapes, the Videophiles (8.7) and Source Shifters (7.5) displayed the highest frequencies. None of the groups viewed many purchased tapes, but the Videophiles had the highest frequency in a relative comparison.

Three types of statistical analysis were used to generate the information presented in the following section. First, a series of one-way analyses of variance were run to determine whether there were differences across the segments on motives for buying and attitudes about using VCRs, time spent with their VCRs advert avoidance behaviours and demographics. Second, correlation coefficients were computed between the length of VCR ownership and measures of TV exposure as well as advert avoidance. Finally, two discriminant analyses were conducted in order to profile the segments psychographically. The first of these examined the key differences between the Time Shifters and the Source Shifters, while the second determined the important differences between the Videophiles and the Low Users.

The Time Shifters were more likely than Source Shifters to be self-controlled. They valued their freedom and personal happiness a great deal, and they liked to try new and different things. In contrast, the Source Shifters enjoyed solving complex problems, sought pleasure and inner harmony. They were imaginative and believed computers should serve people but too often end up controlling people.

Some interesting psychographic differences were also found

between the Videophiles and the Low Users. Compared to the Low Users, the Videophiles had a psychographic profile of the upwardly mobile lifestyle, i.e. they felt they were ambitious, courageous, capable, pleasure seeking and adventuresome (they like to do things on the spur of the moment). They were also opinion leaders. In contrast, the Low Users expressed a preference for an intellectual rather than a pleasure-seeking life, and they said that they liked to try new and different things.

This study clearly demonstrated that a rather demographically homogeneous group of VCR users is not at all homogeneous on many important VCR usage patterns, nor on many fundamental lifestyle characteristics. The segmentation could more usefully be based on an amalgam of variables which the researchers refer to as 'technographic'. A technographic segmentation scheme focuses on the motivations, usage patterns and attitude about technology (in this case VCR usage and other media behaviours), as well as measures of a person's fundamental values and lifestyle perspective.

CONCLUSION

Audience segmentation from a psychographic perspective has indicated that the notion of a mass audience for television hides a great deal of potentially valuable information for advertisers and marketing planners. Even audiences that are apparently homogeneous in terms of demographic features may be readily segmented into further types according to their programme choices and psychological characteristics. Viewers' preferences can be explained by considering the differing needs of various audience segments and the gratifications they expect to gain through the viewing experience. This does not mean that demographic profiles are not useful to broadcasters and advertisers. What it does suggest is that psychological profiles of audience segments can make the demographics more useful.

In the new era of rapid media expansion with increased numbers of media outlets – television channels via terrestrial, satellite and cable distribution systems, radio stations, newspapers and magazines – a richer understanding of media audiences will be called for. Understanding viewers' psychological characteristics which include their needs, interests, values, beliefs and attitudes, will provide fresh and more detailed insights into how and why individuals interact with different media outlets, and respond to different kinds of media content. These features of media experience cut across standard physical attribute discriminators such as age, sex, social class and geographical location and provide a more dynamic model of the viewers' involvement with their preferred media.

8 Applications of psychographics: III. Consumer sub-groups

INTRODUCTION

Psychographic research represents a form of market segmentation based upon measures of different psychological attributes of consumers and their perceptions of products. Psychographics includes measures of consumers' needs and motives and expected gratifications from products, as well as indicators of how they perceive themselves and the rest of the world. Psychographic consumer segments cut across those provided by demographics, but are not substitutes for the physical attribute modes of distinguishing between consumer markets.

The last two chapters have shown that psychographics and life-styles can be used to classify general consumer markets as well as those for specific products. The present chapter will examine the use of psychographics within specified demographic segments. Psychographics are best employed in partnership with demographics. One way in which this can be done is by starting out with a specified demographically defined consumer segment, which is then further defined in terms of psychographic categories. The best illustrations of this application of psychological profiling are psychographic segmentations of the women's and elderly markets.

THE WOMEN'S MARKET

Various studies have been made of women's consumer behaviours. These have included attempts to segment the women's market according to their lifestyles. Many studies have begun by making the basic division between working and non-working women. Another fairly recent classification of women has split them into 'Traditional' or 'Modern', usually according to their stated activities, interests or opinions.

Bryant (1977) describes women as either 'Traditional' or 'Expanding Outlook' ('Modern') depending on their attitudes towards topics such as careers and career opportunities. Traditional women think mothers should stay at home and that boys and girls today each have the same opportunities; Expanding Outlook women believe that marriage and career can be combined and that girls' opportunities are very unequal to those offered to boys. At around the same time, Reynolds, Crask and Wells (1977) studied women who preferred traditional versus contemporary marriages. They found differences in attitudes, patterns of media exposure and use of cosmetic products between traditional and modern women and between working and non-working women within each group.

Another group of studies examined the effect of women's basic roles and role preferences on store patronage behaviour. One study found that working women were more likely to be store loyal, shop only on one day of the week, shop in the evening, consult advertising for special buys and take a list to the store (*Editor and Publisher*, 1972). Among these studies was a survey by Anderson, who found that liberated women made more food shopping trips than either non-liberated or undecided women (Anderson, 1972a). But she also found non-liberated women to be less concerned about convenience and speed of shopping. When her sample was classified into working versus non-working women, working women were found to make fewer shopping trips and to be more brand loyal than their non-working counterparts (Anderson, 1972b). Another study found that both working and non-working women shopped more than once a week, but working women were less likely to patronise neighbourhood supermarkets. Husbands of working women were more likely to do major grocery shopping, while husbands of non-working wives were more likely to purchase just a few items (Douglas, 1975).

The effect of lifestyles on choice behaviour has also been studied. Fry and Siller (1970) analysed product and brand choice behaviour and found that product choice does not vary greatly among women of different social classes. Carmen (1974) reported that women who rated the importance of the maternal role lower than the average were more brand loyal. He suggested that this finding was a consequence of store loyalty since this same group of women also showed higher store loyalty. Anderson (1971) found that the stage in the family life cycle (specifically the presence of two or more pre-teenage children) was more closely associated with the purchase of convenience foods than either social class or income level. One study found that working women are more likely to buy frozen foods than are non-working women (*Editor and Publisher*, 1972), but another study reported an opposite finding (Anderson, 1972b).

At around the same time, Ziff (1971) conducted psychographic research among housewives in America and found a six-fold typology. A sample of 2000 were given 214 attitudinal statements from which the six types were derived. This classification comprised:

(1) *Outgoing Optimists* who were outgoing, innovative, community oriented, positive towards grooming, not bothered by delicate health, digestive problems or especially concerned about germs or cleanliness.

(2) *Conscientious Vigilants* who were conscientious, rigid, meticulous, germ-fighting with a high cleanliness orientation and sensible attitudes about food. They had high cooking pride, a careful shopping orientation and tended not to be convenience oriented.

(3) *Apathetic Indifferents* who were not outgoing, uninvolved with family, irritable, had a negative grooming orientation and were lazy, especially in terms of cooking pride.

(4) *Self-Indulgents* who were relaxed, permissive, unconcerned with health problems, interested in convenience items but with relatively high cooking pride and self-indulgent towards themselves and their families.

(5) *Contented Cows* who were relaxed, not worried, relatively unconcerned about germs and cleanliness, not innovative or outgoing, strongly economy oriented and not self-indulgent.

(6) *Worriers* who were irritable, concerned about health, germs and cleanliness, negative about grooming and breakfast, but self-indulgent with a low economy and high convenience orientation.

Satow and Johnson (1977) classified 1680 women as either full-time housewives or working women and then subclassified working women either as 'Satisfaction Seekers' (career oriented) or 'Income Seekers' (working out of necessity). It is not surprising that they found the full-time housemaker to be traditional in outlook and most involved in the roles of mother and homemaker. This group was most likely to use a list when shopping for groceries and to economise in the supermarket. The Satisfaction Seeker is the most active, liberal and modern. These women indulged in more impulse buying and more meals away from home. The Income Seeker is most concerned about nutrition, but reported the highest usage of convenience foods.

In a study of the relationships between attitudes towards food preparation and food shopping behaviour, Roberts and Wortzel

(1979) uncovered two role orientations among women: traditional and contemporary. Women who are oriented towards traditional roles were hypothesised to exhibit traditional attitudes towards meal preparation and food shopping. They in fact turned out to believe that financial matters should be left to men and for themselves preferred the role of homemaker to that of wage-earner. Contemporary women believed in the sharing of household chores and decisions concerning the home between men and women. They felt that women should be given equality of opportunity in the occupational sphere. The contemporary woman was also concerned with saving time, and felt that they never had enough time to get things done.

Roberts and Wortzel also segmented their women respondents according to their stated food preparation orientations. This analysis yielded five types. The *Joy of Cooking* type was concerned with good cooking and creating new and unusual dishes. The *Service Role* type was motivated by the desire to please their family by preparing good meals and a willingness to spend time doing so. The *Anti-Cooking* type was interested in meals that could be prepared quickly or eaten outside the home to avoid the disliked and time-consuming tasks of cooking and cleaning up. The *Sensory Orientation* described a type who likes to use spices, herbs, wines and sauces to prepare a variety of unusual dishes and meals. Finally, the *Food is Fuel* type held a pragmatic concern for the healthful, nutritional aspects of food rather than its sensory or creative cooking aspects. A further segmentation of women was made in terms of their shopping goals. This yielded three types: *Concern for Time* type who indicated it is important to finish shopping as quickly as possible; *Concern for Price* type who indicated that saving money and budgeting are important; and a *Concern for Quality* type.

These various typologies were then correlated with each other in order to distinguish the character of the traditional woman and the contemporary woman in terms of their food preparation and shopping orientations. The traditional woman tended to be of the *Service Role* and *Food is Fuel* types, while eschewing the views of the *Anti-Cooking* types. In sum, the traditional woman exhibited an orientation towards being a dutiful wife and mother. *Traditional* women however do not cook for pleasure, but do so out of a sense of responsibility to provide satisfying and nutritious meals for their families. *Contemporary* women tended to be oriented towards the *Anti-Cooking* and *Joy of Cooking* points of view. While appearing contradictory there is an explanation for this result. Although many women's attitudes towards their basic roles have changed, it appears that there is still scope for two apparently distinct opinions about cooking. One embodies a total dislike for the activity; the other represents an enjoyment of cooking, not as a proper thing for a woman to do, but as something which when done well can bring intrinsic satisfaction.

Turning next to shopping, traditional women were concerned with quality and somewhat with price minimisation, but were not bothered at all about the time taken up. The traditional woman, it seems, wants to provide high quality food for her family at a reasonable cost, with little concern about the shopping and meal preparation time required. The contemporary woman was concerned principally with saving time.

A further psychographic-style segmentation of women was reported by Bowles (1987), who discussed case studies from the UK and USA. The UK sample was derived from BMRB's Target Group Index (TGI) which has provided continuous information from a single source since 1969 on product usage and media exposure. Its aim is to improve the efficiency of marketing operations by helping advertisers to identify, describe and reach target groups for advertising and other promotional activity.

Apart from the base information on product usage and media, the 24 000 people taking part in TGI each year also complete a battery of 200 attitude statements covering a variety of aspects of their personal and family lives. These attitude statements provide additional insight into the values and motivations of the sample. Cross-analysis of these attitudes with the product and media data, enables marketing researchers to place different consumer groups under the microscope to gain a better impression of how they think and behave.

An increasingly popular use of the TGI database involves a segmentation of the survey respondents based not upon their product usage, but upon their values and attitudes. The cluster analysis technique which underlies the segmentation requires the selection of a number of attitude statements which are employed as the basis for grouping people with similar attitudes together.

Case study one, using UK TGI data, computed a cluster analysis of women aged 15–44 based on their attitudes to appearance, fashion, exercise and health. This analysis resulted in the emergence of six mutually exclusive groups, each group united by a similarity of attitude on different aspects of looks, fashion, health and exercise. The groups were:

(1) *Self-Aware*: hyped on appearance, fashion and exercise.
(2) *Fashion-Directed*: hyped on appearance, not on exercise and sport.
(3) *Green Goddesses*: hyped on sport and fitness, warm on appearance.
(4) *Unconcerned*: neutral attitudes to health and appearance.
(5) *Conscience Stricken*: no time for themselves, busy with responsibilities.
(6) *Dowdies*: dismissive on fashion, cool on exercise and dress for comfort.

These groups were defined without any specific reference to any aspect of product usage or purchasing behaviour, though they were found to be differentially related to product usage, shopping behaviour and demographic character. They were also quite different in their propensity to buy different types of products. The Self-Aware and Fashion-Directed were much heavier users of all cosmetic products than the other attitude groups. The Dowdies used these products least of all, by a long way.

These attitudinally defined groups differed widely in their shopping behaviour, particularly with regard to fashion outlets. The Self-Aware and Fashion-Directed were much more frequent visitors to most fashion outlets, with the exception of C&A. These differences were much more marked with respect to leading-edge fashion retailers.

There were also demographic differences, mainly in terms of age and social class, between attitude clusters. Age differences between the attitude/lifestyle groups were most marked, with the groups having less interest in issues of health and appearance tending to be older in profile. Increasingly, however, the Green Goddesses, who are the most concerned about health issues and exercise, but less fashion aware had fewer younger members.

How well does lifestyle predict product usage compared with demographics? The basis of comparison was with age, since this was the most marked demographic discriminator. It was apparent that both age and lifestyle groups were powerful discriminators of product usage. For age, the index was twice as high in the 15–19 age group as in the 35–44 age group. Discrimination among the lifestyle groups was even greater, with the index being ten times as high for the Self-Aware as for the Dowdies (but it should also be noted that more lifestyle groups than age groups were compared). What is not clear is the extent to which those variations are independent. Do lifestyle differences correlate with age differences? An interlaced analysis demonstrated that not only was lifestyle a more powerful discriminator than age within the 15–44 age range, but that the effects of lifestyle/ attitude and age are relatively independent.

In the second case study, TGI segmentation using attitudinal data, focused on younger women. The data and analysis were provided by the Simmons Market Research Bureau (SMRB), which is BMRB's sister company in the USA. For some years Simmons had been developing a segmentation which would identify those people who really dominate the markets for premium products and services. Early attempts to identify this influential group were based upon household income. It was found that gross income was not the best indicator of spending behaviour. High income households often have such high financial commitments for housing costs, school fees and support of dependents that they have little discretionary income to spend.

Several attempts to develop reliable measures of disposable income suggested that it was extremely difficult to make adequate adjustment for the host of relevant variables such as local and state taxes, housing and living costs, support of dependent parents, etc. After extensive experimentation, Simmons decided to identify the high spender group, not in terms of income, but directly in terms of their ownership or purchasing of a range of high consumer goods and services. People qualified as members of the high spender group if they passed a threshold level for the ownership or purchase of a number of these key items. This group was named the *Get Set* group.

An analysis of the 1985 Simmons survey showed that the Get Set group represented 15 per cent of the projected adult population. Their influence upon the market far outweighs their size however: they have a high propensity to spend. Earnings in Get Set households confirm the important distinction between income and propensity to spend. While all of the Get Set live in households with incomes over $35 000 per annum, only half of them live in households with incomes of over $50 000, the level traditionally denoting the affluence threshold in the USA.

The Simmons database classifies survey respondents in terms of VALS. Just three of the nine VALS lifestyle groups account for almost the whole of the Get Set group. These are Achievers (53.4 per cent), Societally Conscious (28.6 per cent) and Experientials (5.9 per cent). All other VALS groups account for just 12.1 per cent. Despite the high correlation between the VALS groups and membership of the Get Set group, VALS is not a substitute for the spending classification. Roughly 60 per cent of the Achievers and Societally Conscious, and 80 per cent of the Experientials are not included in the Get Set households. There is obviously a gap between aim and achievement.

What else about the Get Set? The Get Set are enthusiastic travellers for holiday and business purposes. While they represent only 15 per cent of the adult population, they account for a quarter of all domestic holidays and a much higher proportion of both holidays abroad and business trips. They are more frequent and dominant members of flying programmes, which enable them to obtain air travel at preferential rates. The Get Set are almost twice as likely to buy a new US-made car than the rest of the population. This contrast increases for imported cars where they are four times as likely to buy. The Get Set also dominate the country in the market for financial services – particularly in connection with stocks and shares.

In conclusion, Bowles (1987) argued that lifestyle classifications can provide valuable additional insights about consumer target groups, but that they are most advantageous when developed to suit particular markets or products.

THE ELDERLY

The over-55s are becoming increasingly important to advertisers. Statistics alone underscore the growing appeal of this market. The number of people in this age bracket is expanding and they are becoming wealthier with more disposable income. Senior citizens typically have greater discretionary income than their younger counterparts, who are considered to be a 'more attractive' market by many businesses. In fact discretionary income coupled with the fact that the older end of the age spectrum consists of people who are healthier and more active makes this market segment an extremely attractive proposition for many commodity and service advertisers.

Many businesses have become firmly entrenched in this market, while others are developing new products and services as well as adapting marketing strategies to make their offerings more appealing to older customers. But there is considerable debate among advertisers and academics about how best to take advantage of these new marketing opportunities. Moreover, there is a very real problem in determining how to reach the senior citizens. With respect to media strategy, a critical consideration is that media usage by the elderly, as a group, is low compared to other demographic groups. As for creative strategy, a paramount question is whether it is more appropriate to view older consumers as constituting one market or several market segments.

The issue of whether the elderly, especially those beyond retirement age, comprise one fairly homogeneous market or several heterogeneous segments has recently received a great deal of attention in the business/professional press. More and more, a segmentation approach is recommended, though there are differences in opinion on the most meaningful basis for segmentation. Lazer (1985), for example, suggests looking at the 'mature market' as comprising four different age groups: 55 to 64, 65 to 74, 75 to 84 and over 85. Other authors (Vivabharanthy and Rink, 1984) suggest combining age breakdowns with other characteristics such as income, education or personality. Still others (e.g. Keane, 1985) recommend the use of lifestyle or psychographic variables in order to achieve a better understanding of the diversity of sub-segments among the elderly.

The very real possibility that there may be distinct segments of the elderly market has important implications for advertisers trying to reach all or some portion of this market. Research findings that provide some additional insights into the viability of taking a segmentation approach come from three areas – gerontology, marketing and communications.

Much of the empirical work in gerontology has led to the identification of different types of people comprising the older age segments. The profiles of these different types tend to be rooted in the manner in which people adjust or adapt to advancing age, and often the descriptions of the different types are similar to personality profiles. While there is considerable agreement in the gerontological literature that there are different types of adjustment patterns among the aged, no clear inference that these different types constitute distinct market segments can be drawn.

Academics and practitioners in marketing have been more directly concerned with answering this question. However, there have been relatively few empirical investigations of the issue. From the studies that have been published though, some support has been produced for the view that there is sufficient heterogeneity among the elderly to justify a segmentation approach.

The communications literature is replete with studies relating to reaching senior citizens, although these studies have typically dealt with older persons as one (more or less homogeneous) group. For example, Steiner (1963) found that when elderly respondents were asked what media types were most important to them, they indicated newspapers, television and radio, in that order. In addition, these respondents perceived television to be an entertainment medium and newspapers an information medium. More recently, Stephens (1982) studied media habits among the elderly and compared her results with those of Steiner. She found that senior citizens seemed to place far more emphasis on television now than on newspapers, but the remainder of Steiner's findings were supported.

Results of another study (Bernhardt and Kinnear, 1976) provided more insight into television viewing habits. For example, the elderly were relatively heavy viewers of daytime television and viewing declined sharply after 10.00 pm. In a different vein, researchers have investigated the sensory processing of the media by senior citizens. Not surprisingly, the findings typically reveal that the elderly, because of decreasing visual acuity, process visual stimuli more slowly than their younger counterparts.

Day, Davis, Dove and French (1988) conducted a study which addressed two specific questions: (1) Is there empirical support for a segmentation approach within the elderly cohort? (2) If there appears to be distinct segments within the cohort, can those segments be reached effectively and efficiently? If so, how, i.e. through what media and what kinds of messages? Day *et al.* decided to experiment with lifestyle measures. The sample they selected consisted of 111 married females over 65 who were not working outside the home. They were given 137 attitude, interest and opinion items. Following factor analysis this set was reduced to 21. Cluster analysis performed on the 21 psychographic variables yielded a two-cluster solution. Then, a second cluster analysis was performed on activity items only and this resulted in the two primary groups being divided into two, yielding four groups in all.

The two major groups were designated the *Self-Sufficient* and the *Persuadables*. The first group exhibited a degree of self-sufficiency that reflected internal locus of control. This manifests itself in risk taking. The second group is more marked by an apparent suscepti-bility to persuasion – more akin to external locus of control.

Within the *Self-Sufficient* group one of the two sub-groups comprised the *Active Integrated* – self-perceived opinion leaders who give rather than request information when interacting with others. They are affluent to the point of feeling capable of handling most situations which entail costs and expenses. Their confidence in their own decision-making ability is not overwhelmed by current social pressures. As well as being opinionated they are also politically conservative.

This segment corresponds closely to Neugarten and associates' 'focused' and 'reorganiser' categories, members of which are charac-terised as perceiving themselves as competent to make decisions and handle life. They generally are better educated than other segments and believe that success comes primarily from hard work. If they worked outside the home, they tended to demonstrate more nurturant and achievement-oriented rather than aggressive traits. In retirement they physically enjoy life and are the most apt of the four sub-groups to try new products.

Members of the second sub-group, the *Disengaged Integrated*, express opinions similar to the *Active Integrated* group. But these people live within a more limited income. While less active than the first segment, their self-confidence carries them through most situations which they face; the one notable exception being handling financial pressures. They do entertain friends in their home and will enjoy a social drink. Generally the Disengaged are quite content with their lives. They are not social isolates. Self-directed, they are interested in more than their daily routine and keep abreast of what is happening in the world.

The two segments of the *Persuadables* can be differentiated along several characteristics. One segment, the *Passive Dependent*, shows a resignation to life that approaches apathy. Not only are they subdued but also have no desire to 'stand out'. New social contacts are minimal and they are content to make their homes the centre of their entire life. Their concern about their physical appearance is an afterthought, at best. They are generally unassertive and generally unconcerned about matters outside the home. They neither care for nor adjust well to major changes, relying for the most part on long-established behavioural patterns and habits. Members of this group usually have not worked outside the home and are at best only moderately satisfied with life.

Unfulfilled desires reflect the character of people in the second sub-group of the *Persuadables*. The *Defended Constricted* are highly sociable, seek acceptance and have the financial means to satisfy desires, especially those desires for something new and different. What they lack is the self-confidence to complete the actions to fulfil those desires. They are somewhat averse to risk, and seek assurance from others that they are indeed doing the wise thing. Their social orientation is a function of the fear that being homebound will cause them to miss the interesting facets of life. They tend to be preoccupied with health and/or trying to continue with the activities they enjoyed during middle life. Moreover they try to sustain a high level of activity and to like activity outside the home in order to ward off the image of incapacity due to ageing. Day *et al.* (1988) suggest that this information about elderly characteristics can guide advertisers in deciding upon campaign strategies to employ in respect of particular commodities.

With respect to creative strategy, messages directed at members of the *Self-Sufficient* group, for example, should reflect their internal locus of control. That is, they should be portrayed as self-confident, independent and outgoing. In order to design advertisements to which these people can easily relate, scenarios might show these people as leading active lifestyles, e.g., entertaining friends, attending events outside the home, and looking the part of sociable, up-to-date individuals. In contrst, people in the *Persuadable* group are more likely to relate to scenarios centred on activities in and around the home.

For advertisers who want to target their messages more narrowly, the profiles of the four sub-groups suggest ways of doing so. For example, those people in the *Active Integrated* segment are more self-confident and therefore more self-reliant in their decision making. They are more satisfied with their financial status and somewhat more adventurous. Hence, not only should the advertising reflect this self-confidence, but it should also provide factual information to enable this segment to make their own decisions. In contrast, the *Disengaged Integrated* women tend to seek advice from others when making decisions, so advertising depicting people seeking advice and information from significant others is more likely to be effective in communicating the selling message to this segment.

The two subsets of the *Persuadable* group also offer contrasts that can be useful in designing advertising messages. For example, those people in the *Passive Dependent* segment tend to fit the traditional old-age stereotype. That. is, they are more conservative, more emotionally dependent and more risk-averse than those people in the *Defended Constricted* segment. Moreover, the *Passive Dependent* are 'homebodies' and rarely venture out, whereas the *Defended Constricted* are much more sociable and active. While the advertiser would not want to portray the *Passive Dependent* as dullards, sensitivity to their insecurities and lack of social contact can increase the effectiveness of advertising messages.

Market segmentation information about the elderly can guide media strategies as well. Day *et al.* (1988) noted a number of interesting differences between lifestyle groups in their media usage habits and preferences. *Self-Sufficient* people were considerably heavier readers of magazines, whereas those in the *Persuadable* group watched more television. In particular, the *Self-Sufficient* read a variety of women's and health magazines, reflecting that they are more cosmopolitan. The travel section of the newspaper and travel magazines are appropriate places to get their attention. Not too surprisingly, neither group is likely to read business magazines. The Persuadables read little in any case.

Davis and French (1989) also explored ways of segmenting the elderly market. The objectives of the study were:

(1) To identify potential audience segments among the elderly, based primarily on attitudes toward advertising.

(2) To develop psychographic profiles for each of these potential audiences in order to provide insight on the make-up of these individuals and to facilitate comparison of results to those found in previous studies.

(3) To examine media consumption among these audiences to determine whether the diversity identified with respect to information usage is reflected in media habits.

The study used a sample of 217 married female respondents aged 60 and over. Respondents were asked to rate agreement with over 200 psychographic statements, which dealt with a variety of attitudes, opinions and interests. They were also questioned about their sources of information about brands and products and their beliefs about advertising. Three distinct segments of elderly females were identified based on advertising attitudes and beliefs: *Engaged, Autonomous* and *Receptive.*

Engaged agreed that advertising insulted her intelligence and did not believe a company's advertisement when it claimed that test results showed its product to be better than competing products. She often sought the advice of friends regarding brands and products and agreed that information from advertising helped her make better buying decisions. In sharp contrast to the other two groups, these women relied upon the opinions of others in evaluating products. The level of social activity of these women makes it clear that they have not disengaged from society as some elderly tend to do.

Autonomous did not seek out the advice of friends regarding brands and products and was neutral about the value of information from advertising in making purchase decisions. These women also felt that advertising insulted their intelligence and were highly suspicious of competitive advertisements. These individuals did not seem to rely heavily on any external sources for information. They apparently relied more upon personal experience as an internal information source.

Receptive did not believe that advertising insulted her intelligence, thereby differing from women in the first two segments. While she was suspicious of competitive advertising, she believed that advertising helped her make better buying decisions. While these individuals seemed to utilise and rely on information from advertising, they did not tend to consult with friends about brands and products. The attitudes these women held towards advertising made this group a more receptive audience for advertisers.

Four psychographic profiles emerged following analysis of responses to the psychographic statements. These were:

(1) a cosmopolitan dimension;
(2) importance of cooking and baking;
(3) combination of innovativeness and concerns for personal and social issues;
(4) negative outlook on business in general.

Engaged segment members would seem to be of special interest to companies introducing new products for elderly consumers. This group was more innovative than either of the other segments. The task of reaching this segment is aided by their media habits. This group uses mass media to a considerable extent, especially news media. In addition, they are socially involved and often consult with friends regarding products. This might aid in disseminating new product knowledge through word-of-mouth communication.

Autonomous segment members were the least innovative of the three groups and would not be as attractive as targets for new products. They do not use mass media as heavily as those in the *Engaged* segment and seem to be more socially isolated.

Receptive segment members are a particularly attractive target for those businesses which rely on advertising to communicate with prospects. These women display fairly favourable attitudes towards advertising and business. Of special note is their use of television comedy programmes. Comedic appeals might be appropriate in reaching this group. Advertising done in connection with TV comedy programmes would probably be more effective in reaching this group than either of the other two segments.

Gollub and Javitz (1989) reported a national US study of how older adults prefer to live in retirement. The study – Lifestyles and Values of Older Adults (LAVOA) – was sponsored by the National Association for Senior Living Industries (NASLI) and conducted by SRI International. The study was commissioned to provide a better understanding of how older adults think, and how they differ from one another. It revealed six older-adult market segments defined by psychological, demographic and health factors. Each segment of older adults differs in how it wants to live in retirement. Some want to live in single-family homes, while others want independent apartments, congregate-care facilities or life-care communities. Congregate-care facilities are retirement housing complexes that offer residents a variety of on-site services, including meals, for a monthly fee. Life-care communities offer unlimited care until death, including on-site nursing homes, for an entry fee. Some older adults want community and recreational amenities, and convenience and health services, while others are not interested in services, preferring to remain independent.

In a survey of 3600 nationally representative people aged 55 and older, SRI identified four psychological factors that influence these preferences. First, autonomy–dependence – the degree to which people are driven by the need to be on their own. Second, introversion–extroversion – the degree to which people are outer-directed and seek social involvement. Third, self-indulgence/self-denial – how much people seek gratification. Fourth, resistance/openness to change – how adaptable people are. The SRI analysis also examined the health status of older Americans to determine how much people's functional ability affects their lifestyle preferences, apart from psychological or socio-economic factors.

Six distinct psychographic segments of older adults emerged from the study: (1) Explorers, (2) Adapters, (3) Pragmatists, (4) Attainers, (5) Martyrs and (6) Preservers. Each segment has a distinct psychology and distinct preferences for how it wants to live in retirement. Gollub and Javitz provided a descriptive biographical synopsis for each type.

Explorers want to do things their way. They are self-reliant and less willing than any other segment to believe children have an obligation to assist their parents. They are also the most introverted segment, reflecting their individualism. This segment is in moderately better health, is slightly younger and is somewhat better educated than older adults as a whole. Explorers' rugged individualism reflects life experiences that taught them self-reliance; they have less faith in the ability of others to meet their needs. Their autonomy and tendency towards self-denial may reflect a distrust of institutions and poor self-image.

Adapters are the most extrovert segment and they are also open to change. But no other segment except Preservers is more dependent. Adapters are the socialites among their peers. Personal relationships and material possessions play an important role in their sense of well-being. Along with Attainers, Adapters have the highest level of education, and they are second only to the same segment in self-indulgence, health and wealth. Adapters are less willing to believe that children have an obligation to assist their parents than are older adults as a whole. Adapters are more likely than the average older American to live with a spouse and children, and to like where they live, but they have also thought about moving. They are more inclined than the average to consider moving to an apartment. They rank second among the six segments (following Attainers) in their interest in moving to a better climate and changing to a new lifestyle.

Pragmatists are the second most extroverted segment (following Adapters), the second most willing to agree that children have an obligation to assist their parents (following Martyrs), the second oldest (following Preservers) and the third most self-indulgent (following Adapters and Attainers). Pragmatists are also slightly less well educated and wealthy, but healthier than the older adult population as a whole. They are average in their dependence and openness to change. Pragmatists are conservative and conformist in their values. While they are self-indulgent, their sense of well-being depends more than other segments on how they are perceived. They are also more family centred than the other segments.

Pragmatists are the second most likely group to live alone, the least likely to have thoughts about moving and the second most likely to think about moving to a nursing home, an older-adult housing complex, or to get help in caring for themselves. They are not interested in moving to an adult community, though they rank second in their concern about having social supports, and rank first in wanting to live with people of the same religion.

Among all the segments, *Attainers* are the youngest, most autonomous, self-indulgent, healthy and wealthy. Along with Adapters, they have the best education, and they are second only to Adapters in their openness to change. Next to Explorers, Attainers are the least willing to believe that children have an obligation to help their parents. This segment is average in its introversion/extroversion. Attainers are more impulse oriented than the other segments, and more capable of realising their objectives. Their values are oriented toward getting what they want.

Attainers are the most likely to own their own homes, the most likely to live with their spouse and the most likely to have children living at home. They are the least likely to want to move to an adult community with a service package. They are most likely to have thought of moving – particularly to another state – to a smaller home, to get cash from their current home or to live in a better climate with a new lifestyle and fewer chores. They are more likely to want children to be included in any community where they live, and they care about having movie theatres, cultural events, parks and colleges on site nearby.

Martyrs are resistant to change. This is the segment that most agrees that children should help their parents. Though martyrs are the second youngest segment next to Attainers, they are second only to Preservers in being the least well educated, the most self-denying, the least wealthy and the least healthy. They are second only to Explorers in being introverted. Martyrs stand out because they are less able to express and implement their values than the other segments (though they are not the poorest, or the least healthy group). They rationalise their helplessness through denial and introversion.

Martyrs are more likely than the other segments to live with their children or relatives, or to find their current home too hard to maintain and to want to leave the community. They are the segment most likely to want to move to a larger home, to want to move closer to shops and to consider moving to an adult community.

Preservers are by far the least healthy segment – almost all the survey respondents with serious health problems fell into this category. Preservers are second only to Martyrs in their resistance to change. They are highly need-driven compared with the other segments – their concern is with preserving what they have, and they have little. They look to helpers, whether family or professionals, to maintain their quality of life.

Preservers are the segment most likely to rent an apartment or live in older-adult housing in a high-rise building. They are most likely to live alone, or with children or relatives. They are the most likely to consider moving to older-adult housing, and they are most likely to feel that security, central dining, meal delivery, maid, maintenance and housekeeping services are essential in retirement housing.

CONCLUSION

Psychographics has been used to segment many markets for many different products and services. As new markets have emerged such as women's products and the elderly, so psychographic techniques have been applied to them. What is perhaps most interesting is that although very different psychographic categories have emerged for different populations and products, there are remarkable similarities between them. Clearly there are other potentially wealthy groups that merit psychographic attention. These include the ethnic minorities and the young.

9 Putting psychographics into practice

INTRODUCTION

The psychology of market segmentation embodies a number of marketing research techniques. Principal among them is that the practical application of the behavioural and social sciences to marketing, which has come to be known as psychographics. As the preceding chapters have shown, psychographics is only one among several important market segmentation methods, all of which can supply marketers with valuable information to guide strategic marketing decisions, if used appropriately.

Psychographics was pioneered by Emanuel Demby, but has since been developed by many other marketing researchers in academia and the commercial world. Psychographics does not represent a single instrument but has evolved out of the practical application of personality and lifestyle research. Thus, psychographics is related both to individuals' personality traits and their lifestyles. The latter are mainly and usually defined in terms of attitudes, interests and opinions.

Psychographics was introduced under the broader heading of 'behavioural segmentation'. Other behavioural segmentation techniques include product usage segmentation and benefit segmentation. These, along with physical attribute segmentations (e.g., geodemographics), should not be conceived as being mutually exclusive in practical marketing situations. Any and all of these types of market segmentation can provide the marketing planner with helpful data, and used together in the right way they can prove to be a powerful mix. This chapter will begin to review the advantages and disadvantages of psychological or behavioural modes of market segmentation. Some guidelines will be offered for putting psychographics and other behavioural segmentation methods into practice. Finally, a look is taken at some interesting new developments in the application of psychological variables to market segmentation.

ADVANTAGES OF PSYCHOGRAPHICS

Psychographic research is being more frequently used in market segmentation studies for four primary reasons: (1) to identify target markets; (2) to provide better explanations of consumer behaviour; (3) to improve a company's strategic marketing efforts; (4) To minimise risks for new products and business ventures. We can take a look at each of these advantages in turn.

Identifying target markets

Although typically used more in advanced analysis than initial segmentation studies, psychographics can be very useful in identifying and explaining the behaviour of markets. Consumer differences extend beyond demographics and research must probe into an individual's state of mind (their personality and their lifestyle) in order to understand the way consumers interact with the marketplace. For example, although the market for cars can be defined in geodemographic terms, psychographically a researcher may be able to identify many reasons or motives underlying car buying behaviour which could help to design a more effective promotional and marketing strategy. Some consumers may choose their car on the basis of price, but others may be influenced by the style and colour, by how they perceive it will project a certain image, or make a certain statement about themselves. Other consumers may give most weight to reliability, and yet others may be swayed by the nationality of the model. Psychographic analysis can provide marketers with a more complete profile of the target market for a product.

Consumer behaviour

Markets are made up of a variety of people. By analysing consumer behaviour, the marketer can better understand why buyers act as they do in the marketplace. Psychographic research can assist in meeting this objective. Buyer behaviour – including such factors as brand choice, store/firm loyalty, personal motivations, attitudes, perceptions and preferences – can all be explored via this approach to segmentation. The value of such information is readily apparent.

A company may know who the heavy users of their product are, but not why these individuals act as they do. Through psychographic research, the firm can study this small core with high specific consumption patterns to determine what they like about the product and why they buy it. This information can then be used in designing future promotional appeals to this group, as well as offering similar benefits to potential new users. Is the shopper who regularly patronises a particular supermarket going there because it is the most convenient one, because of its fine meat and produce departments or for other reasons?

Strategic marketing

The additional marketing information available through psychographic analysis can be employed in planning successful marketing strategies for the firm. Psychographics is most useful for companies that sell:

- expensive products (cars, boats).
- discretionary goods or services (VCRs, social club membership).
- somewhat indistinguishable products (soft drinks, petrol, beer, spirits).

Strategic information gathered through a psychographic analysis can permeate all marketing areas of the company. Some examples include:

- positioning new products/repositioning existing products.
- improving products or services to better meet segment needs.
- recognising the importance of price factors in a given market.
- promotional strategies, in particular selecting appropriate media.
- vehicles, advertising messages and sales appeals.
- exploring new distribution methods or improving existing channels of distribution.

Minimising risk

The cost of a new production, brand line extension or proposed venture can be substantial. Furthermore, the vast majority of such products fail (new product success rates are estimated at less than 10 per cent). By incorporating psychographic research into a company's product testing and development programme, project successes become more likely. Often the key ingredient is locating the subtle product or concept variations that consumers desire (their needs and wants).

GENERAL GUIDELINES FOR PRACTITIONERS

The success or failure of any market segmentation exercise may hang crucially on the effectiveness and care with which it is implemented and applied. This book has been about psychographic segmentation, though the reader will have learned that this form of market segmentation is best considered in the broader context of other forms of classifying consumers. Marketing research is becoming an increasingly complex business. In the field of market segmentation, techniques are advancing all the time. Despite this development, however, there is, as yet, no one preferred format or approach when conducting a psychographic segmentation study. Users should therefore bear in mind a number of helpful rules of thumb when moving into this area.

First, lifestyles are themselves a complex subject. Marketing measures based on lifestyle variables will only be of any real use to the extent that they obtain data that are relevant to the particular marketing problem being investigated. It can be advantageous, technically and financially, to begin any new psychographic research with a qualitative phase, comprising focus groups or individual depth interviews, to ensure that the concepts and language used in the quantitative survey phase are relevant and meaningful.

Second, when obtaining lifestyle data, personal, face-to-face interviews represent the best method, even though they can be more costly than postal or telephone surveys. Postal surveys often produce poor return rates, while interviews conducted on the telephone have the disadvantage of not allowing for any possible visual illustration of items, which can sometimes help respondents understand better what they are being asked.

Third, the best psychographic instruments are those whose items are meaningfully associated with the consumer behaviour being addressed. Activity, interest and opinion statements work best when they are related to the purchase decision. Not only is the wording of these statements important, however, but also the range of response options. Some industry experts have recommended that five-point agree–disagree scales be used alongside each item. Others, however, have argued that more response points work better. A wider scale allows for greater dispersion from the mid-point, and such deviations from the centre or average underlie the determination of segment formation. Thus, clear and distinct segments may be more likely to emerge from more detailed psychographic scales.

Fourth, it is important to try to avoid preconceived notions about the research findings. In addition to setting research objectives, it is also useful to develop some research hypotheses prior to conducting the research. This forces some consideration of the consequences and implications of the possible findings. However, it is often necessary to be open-minded about the outcome of a study. While psychographics can often yield results which are informative and add a new dimension to marketing planning and decision making, sometimes unexpected findings can emerge.

Fifth, additional value can be found in secondary data. A psychographic analysis usually turns up trumps when based on well-executed primary research. This does not mean that secondary data should be ignored. Information from past studies as well as published or syndicated sources can lend further context and perspective to any investigation and contribute significantly to the interpretation of primary research findings.

Finally, it is important to remember that psychographic segmentations need not, and perhaps should not, be used on their own. Combined with pertinent demographic and behavioural segmentation data, psychographics can function as a component of a very powerful market segmentation mix.

SYNDICATED RESEARCH

The above guidelines offer rules of thumb to those marketers who decide to embark on their own, original segmentation research. While having certain advantages, it is not necessary to opt for custom-built psychographic research. There are a number of syndicated lifestyle surveys which provide extensive psychological and lifestyle segmentation data. Two of the best known providers of these services are Yankelovich Clancy Shulman (YCS) and SRI International.

The Yankelovich Monitor 1985 identified 52 social trends relevant to consumer marketing and six value segments. The recognition of the impact of key trends in a given market can prove to be valuable for a company's strategic marketing planning. Generalised typologies, on the other hand, may be more useful in understanding value systems operating in today's commercial environment as a whole, rather than in specific product markets.

SRI's VALS programme (Values and Lifestyles) categorises people based on attitudes, needs, wants and beliefs. The original VALS typology is divided into four major categories, with a total of nine lifestyle types. VALS information has been used in marketing research, advertising, product development, strategic planning, sales and human resource development applications. More recently, SRI have introduced a new VALS system in response to growing dissatisfaction with the strength of links between the original consumer types and purchase behaviours. VALS2 offers an eight-fold typology arranged horizontally as well as vertically. This reflects an arrangement of consumer needs, not simply in a top to bottom fashion, from basic survival level motives to the higher-order, self-fulfilment drives, but a horizontal arrangement indicating whether consumers are driven by principles, status or the desire for action.

Syndicated services such as the Monitor and VALS are growing in popularity. There is, however, some question as to their effectiveness. This form of generalised lifestyle research is market or consumer-driven, as opposed to product-driven. Individuals are analysed as to their overall attitudes, values and desires. Product specific data, the more important information from a market segmentation perspective, is not obtained. Marketers can only infer how consumer segments will respond to their product offerings. The latter information is very important, since consumers respond differently when exposed to different products. Thus, in addition to a general psychological portrait of the consumer world, there is a pressing need for situation-specific data focusing on unique markets, and specific product classes and product items.

SPECIFIC CONCERNS WITH MARKET SEGMENTATION

Segmentation studies have followed one of two prototypical patterns: the first type involves an a priori segmentation design in which corporate management decides on a basis for segmentation such as product purchase, loyalty, customer type or some other factor. The survey results then show each segment's estimated size and their demographic, socio-economic, psychographic and other relevant characteristics. The second type is a clustering-based segmentation design in which segments are determined on the basis of a clustering of respondents on a set of 'relevant' variables. Benefit, need and attitude segmentation are examples of this type of approach. As in a priori segmentation studies, the size and other characteristics (demographic, socio-economic, psychographic, product usage and so on) of the segments are estimated.

Although segmentation studies have been dominated by these two prototypical designs, several major conceptual and methodological developments have been proposed in the academic literature. The advancement of market segmentation research requires, therefore, narrowing the gap between the academically oriented research on segmentation and the real world application of segmentation research. Segmentation studies should be re-evaluated and new designs and analytical approaches considered.

Although using psychographic techniques in segmentation studies can be very beneficial, there are some limitations users must bear in mind, as well as certain features on which careful checks should be made.

Problems in data collection and analysis

Problems may be experienced during the data collection stage of marketing segmentation research, especially when psychographic techniques are being used, because psychographics requires a more complex and sensitive approach to obtaining marketing information than, for example, demographics. Psychographic data also require a more sophisticated type of analysis to put them into an interpretable and usable form.

Although the psychographic study is simpler to administer than in-depth interviews (previously the most popular means of obtaining lifestyle information), data collection is often a problem due to the large number of questions asked via the survey instrument. Compounding this situation is the analysis of a voluminous amount of data, which often requires the use of more advanced multivariate statistical techniques in seeking key marketing relationships. In some cases, the results of the research may prove inconclusive. This can present problems in finding significant differences between market segments or producing too many variations among segments. In the latter case of over-segmentation, a market combination strategy might be advisable. This involves the combination of two or more small segments into a larger one that is more efficient for marketing planning purposes.

Data reliability

Despite the importance of assuring that segmentation analysis is conducted on reliable data, little attention is paid to this issue in most segmentation (and marketing) studies, and the data analysed are assumed to be reliable. Some variables (e.g., demographic characteristics) are more reliable than others (e.g., attitudes and psychographic characteristics). Whenever there is reason to suspect the reliability of some variables, certain safeguards such as test–re-test reliability measures should be considered.

Segment stability

An often neglected aspect of segmentation research is the question of segment stability over situations and time. Do individuals remain in the same market category over time? To what extent do the size and demographic composition of market segments change? The answers to these questions depend on three sets of factors.

(1) *The basis for segmentation.* In general one might hypothesise that the more specific the basis for segmentation (e.g., price sensitivity or purchase of a given brand) the less stable the segment. Similarly, the more general the basis for segmentation (benefits sought from the product category or needs) the more stable the market.

(2) *The volatility of the marketplace.* Changes in the competitive activities and the environmental (political, legal, cultural, economic, etc.) conditions are likely to disturb the stability of the segments, and increase the likelihood of switching among segments.

(3) *Consumer characteristics.* All consumers go through basic life-cycle changes; even in the short term (within a life-cycle stage) consumers may differ with respect to their likelihood to change and the nature of the change.

The specific variables which operate in each of these three sets of conditions must be identified, and the nature and magnitude of their impact on changes in the stability of various segments (e.g., buyers versus non-buyers, different benefit segments, etc.) must be assessed.

Segment homogeneity

Segmentation studies commonly involve the determination of the segments (based on either a priori judgement or a clustering approach) followed by the identification of the segment profile on the respondents' other characteristics. The latter stage is usually under-taken by examining the possibility of significant differences between segment means on a set of background variables.

Finding that two or more segments are different in terms of their mean profiles does not provide any indication about the possible segments within each segment. Members of a 'buyer' segment, for example, may buy a given brand for different reasons. They may be very heterogeneous in their needs, demographic characteristics and information requirements. In principle, almost every segment may, in turn, be decomposable into sub-segments. Hence, to achieve intra-segment homogeneity, a very specific multidimensional definition of the basis for segmentation is required.

The segmentability of the market

Segmentation studies are based on the premise that the given market is heterogeneous and can therefore be segmented. Most empirical segmentation studies support this premise. It is not uncommon, however, to find markets in which no significant differences are found among various segments with respect to their demographic or other relevant consumer characteristics, such as response elasticities to marketing variables.

Validation

One of the major discrepancies between academic and commercial studies of segmentation is with respect to the question of validity. Whereas many academic studies of segmentation do employ some form of validation, most of the commercially-based segmentation studies ignore the question of validity. The validity question is by far the most crucial one. Do the segments discovered in a segmentation study exist in the population? Is the estimated segment size accurate? Finally, how accurate are the estimated segment responses to the firm's marketing actions?

Data interpretation and implementation of results

Regardless of how sophisticated the segmentation study, the key to a successful project is the researcher's and user's (management's) ability to interpret the results and use them as guidelines for the design, execution and evaluation of appropriate marketing strategy. The data interpretation stage should be jointly performed by the researcher and user, reflecting the researcher's statistical judgements (which differences among segments are statistically significant, etc.) and the manager's product/market knowledge. In this context, the two major issues are how to determine the number of segments and select the largest segment(s) and how to translate the segmentation findings into marketing strategy.

The first issue is a complex issue and is determined by a mixture of segment stability and homogeneity, together with managerial consid-eration of the cost of segmentation. Whatever segmentation approach is used, it is management that selects the desired target segments. The selection of target segments is a complex 'art' and the process should take into account such factors as the segment's expected response to marketing variables, the segment's reachability, the nature of competition activity within the segment, and management's resources and ability to implement a segmented strategy for the selected segment. The cost of segmentation, the problems inherent in any effort to reach effectively a large number of segments and the complexity of managing a large number of segments all encourage the selection of relatively few segments. However, greater segment homogeneity requires a larger number of segments.

The second issue of translating segmentation findings into target selection is equally problematic. The most difficult aspect of any segmentation project is the translation of the study results into marketing strategy. No rules can be offered to assure a successful translation. There are, however, a few generalisable conclusions to be derived from observations of successful and unsuccessful translations.

(1) Involve all the relevant users (e.g., product managers, new product developers, advertising agency personnel, etc.) in the problem definition, research design and data interpretation stages.
(2) View segmentation data as one input to a total marketing information system and combine them with sales and other relevant data.
(3) Use the segmentation data on a continuous basis. The reported study results should be viewed only as the beginning of a utilisation programme.

Difficulties with, and the nature of, the translation of segmentation findings into a strategy depend on whether the segmentation study is used as input to:

(1) idea and strategy generation or strategy evaluation;
(2) product related decisions (i.e. product positioning, design and price) or communication and distribution decisions; or
(3) decisions about existing products (i.e. no change, product modification, repositioning or deletion decisions) or new products.

The translation of segmentation findings into new ideas (and strategies) is usually limited only by the creativity of the users. Most segmentation studies, and especially those based on consumers' needs, benefits, lifestyles or other psychographic characteristics, offer a rich profile of potential target segments which, in turn, can lead to the generation of a large number of diverse ideas and strategies. Furthermore, if one is concerned, for example, with the design of a product or a communication campaign, each idea can be executed in a variety of ways, the success of which depends more on the creativity of the designer than on the segmentation findings.

The translation of segmentation findings is more complex when they are used to evaluate (rather than generate) some marketing strategy. In this context, two situations are distinct: consumer reactions to a new strategy (e.g., new concept or new commercial) and consumer satisfaction with a company's current products and services. In both cases a meaningful evaluation should be done at the market segment level, and in both cases there is a strong tendency to define segments in terms which are favourable to the corporate decision maker's objectives.

A major difficulty in the translation of segmentation findings into actionable strategy is management's perceived ability to implement the strategy. In industrial marketing, it is often argued that salesmen cannot effectively handle simultaneously a number of strategies aimed at a number of market segments. Furthermore, organisations, whether in consumer or industrial markets, are on average reluctant to undertake high risk strategies. Strategies which depart from current practice or which require new ways of reaching target segments (e.g., using new and different media outlets from those customarily utilised) are viewed as high risks. In providing rigorous input to decisions perceived as involving high risks, segmentation findings can have a major impact.

THE GENERALISABILITY OF MARKET SEGMENTATION

Most marketing efforts will be more effective if the consumers' personal values are considered. Adding value information to demographics can greatly enhance the effectiveness of segmentation (Kahle *et al.*, 1989; Perri, 1990; Rousseau, 1990). Psychographic value information can be used by marketers to appeal directly and efficiently to those groups that are the most likely to find their brand appealing. The marketer can also use this information to create new brands to fit patterns their brand cannot satisfy (Wells, 1974).

If the type of psychographic segments are stable across countries, then a multinational company need not perform marketing research in all the countries it operates (providing the company knows the frequency of each segment in each country). This would result in a great reduction of research expenses and this saving could be quite significant.

Psychographic methods are commonly used. A 1977 American Marketing Association survey found that 37.9 per cent of marketing firms surveyed used psychographic research methods frequently (Lesser and Hughes, 1986). Psychographics has been used by Schlitz beer, the Ford Pinto and Merrill Lynch (Wells, 1974). Over 250 companies have used VALS data, including GM, Ford, Nissan, Honda, Mercedes-Benz, AT&T, New York Times, Penthouse, Atlantic Richfield and Boeing Commercial Airplane Company (see Kahle *et al.*, 1986). Lesser and Hughes' 1986 study suggests that psychographic segments developed in one geographic area are generalisable to other areas. Boote's (1981) study also supports a single advertising campaign across countries.

Goodyear Tyre Company has divided its customers into six segments according to psychographic information (Prestige Buyer, Comfortable Conservative, Value Shopper, Pretender, Trusting Patron and Bargain Hunter). Each of these segments have specific value characteristics. Goodyear has found that segment sizes vary between countries, but each segment's profile remains the same (Boole, 1981).

Despite these few examples, there is a need for more cross-cultural research. This cross-cultural research of values would provide a necessary understanding of consumers. Mitchell (1983) using the VALS system attempted to describe how the nine psychographic types differ across five major European industrialised countries and the USA. Precisely how good the data were, is uncertain, but the principle is important. According to this analysis the psychographic types remain constant but the demographic make-up of those types is different. It might be just as likely to conceive of a situation where the psychographic segments themselves do not generalise over regions, countries and continents.

CONCLUSION

Psychographics is neither the panacea for all marketeering woes, nor is it a trivial fad that will pass away. It is based on sensible and sensitive assumptions that by understanding the values and lifestyles of consumers better their behaviour will be more predictable. Some have attempted to segment all markets according to a mixture of attitudes, beliefs, interests, values and lifestyles. Some of these psychographic typologies have been widely accepted and adopted though at least four major alternative classifications exist. Others have argued, wisely, that although it is much more costly and time consuming, predictability goes up with specificity. Hence there are product specific, and sometimes brand specific typologies that make fine segmentations. Naturally these frequently do not translate into other brands though there is some obvious overlap between them.

For many reasons the quality and quantity of psychographic research is patchy. Some organisations who have invested large sums of money into a psychographic segmentation instrument are naturally loath to let potential competitors see it, so excellent examples of psychographic methodology do not come to light. The literature is also scattered across academic, applied and trade journals which makes it difficult to collect and assess. Of course, badly done research, however well it is marketed, will not further the field or fulfil the promise of psychographics.

Psychographics, like psychology itself, has a short history, but a long past, and we predict a good future. There is no doubt that along with other more classic forms of market segmentation, psychographics has an important part to play in marketing strategy and research.

Bibliography

Advertising Research Foundation (1964) *Are There Consumer Types?*, New York: Advertising Research Foundation.

Allsop, J. F. (1986) 'Personality as a determinant of beer and cider consumption among young men', *Personality and Individual Differences*, 7, 341–7.

Alpert, M. I. (1972) 'Personality and the determinants of product choice', *Journal of Marketing Research*, 9, 89–92.

Anderson, B. B. (1972a) 'Are we missing the MS?', *Proceedings of the Third Annual Conference of the Association for Consumer Research*, pp. 436–45.

Anderson, B. B. (1972b) 'Working women versus non-working women: A comparison of shopping behaviours', *Combined Proceedings*, American Marketing Association, pp. 355–9.

Anderson, W. T. Jr. (1971) 'Identifying the convenience oriented customer', *Journal of Marketing Research*, 8, 179–83.

Andreason, A. R. (1984) 'Life status changes and changes in consumer preferences and satisfaction', *Journal of Consumer Research*, 11, 784–94.

Ansbacher, A. L. and Ansbacher, R. (ed.) (1956) *The Individual Psychology of Alfred Adler*, New York: Basic Books.

Arndt, J. (1974) *Market Segmentation*, Bergen, Norway: Universitetsforlaget.

Arnold, S. J. and Tigert, D. J. (1973) 'Canadians and Americans: A comparative analysis', Paper delivered at the Annual Convention of the American Psychological Association, Montreal, Canada.

Atkin, C., Greenberg, B., Korzenny, F. and McDermott, S. (1979) 'Selective exposure to televised violence', *Journal of Broadcasting*, 23, 5–13.

Atkinson, J. W. (1953) 'The achievement motive and recall of interrupted and completed tasks', *Journal of Experimental Psychology*, 46, 381–90.

Atlas, J. (1984) 'Beyond demographics', *Atlantic Monthly*, October, 49–59.

Baker, M. and Gorsuch, R. (1982) 'Trait anxiety and intrinsic–extrinsic religiousness', *Journal for the Scientific Study of Religion*, 21, 119–24.

Bass, F. M. (1974) 'The theory of stochastic preference and brand switching', *Journal of Marketing Research*, 11, 1–20.

Bass, F. M., Pessemeier, E. A. and Tigert, D. J. (1969) 'A taxonomy of magazine readership applied to problems in marketing strategy and media selection', *Journal of Business*, 42, 337–63.

Baumgarten, S. A. (1975) 'The innovative communicator in the diffusion process', *Journal of Marketing Research*, 12, 12–18.

Bearden, W. O., Teel, J. E. Jr. and Durand, R. M. (1978) 'Media usage, psychographics and demographic dimensions of retail shoppers', *Journal of Retailing*, 54, 65–74.

Beatty, S. E., Kahle, L. R., Homer, P. and Shekhar, M. (1985) 'Alternative measurement approaches to consumer values: The list of values and the Rokeach value survey', *Psychology and Marketing*, 2, 181–200.

Becherer, R. C., Morgan, F. W. and Richard, L. M. (1979) 'Person–situation interaction within a consumer behaviour context', *Journal of Psychology*, 102, 235–42.

Behaviour Science Corporation (1972) *Developing the Family Travel Market*, Des Moines, Iowa: Better Homes and Gardens.

Bernay, E. K. (1971) 'Lifestyle analysis as a basis for media selection', in C. King and D. Tigert (eds) *Attitude Research Reaches New Heights*, Chicago: American Marketing Association.

Bernhardt, K. L. and Kinnear, T. C. (1976) 'Profiling the senior citizens' market', in B. Anderson (ed.) *Advances in Consumer Research*.

Berry, L. L. (1969) 'Components of department store image: A theoretical and empirical analysis', *Journal of Retailing*, 51, 3–20.

Blackwell, R. D. and Talarzyk, W. W. (1977) 'Lifestyle retailing; competition strategies for the 1980s', *Journal of Retailing*, 59, 7–27.

Blem, N. H., Reekie, W. D. and Brits, R. N. (1989) *Elements of South African Marketing*, Johannesburg: Southern Book Publications.

Boole, A. S. (1981) 'Market segmentation by personal values and salient product attributes', *Journal of Advertising Research*, 21, 29–35.

Bower, R. T. (1973) *Television and the Public*. New York: Holt, Rinehart & Winston.

Bowers, K. S. (1973) 'Situationism in psychology: An analysis and a critique', *Psychological Review*, 80, 307–36.

Bowles, T. (1987) 'Does classifying people by lifestyle really help the advertisers?', *Admap*, May, 36–40.

Bowman, G. W. and Farley, J. (1972) 'TV viewing: Application of a formal choice model', *Applied Economics*, 4, 245–59.

Boyanowsky, E. O. (1977) 'Film preferences under condition of threat: Whetting the appetite for violence, information or excitement?', *Communication Research*, 1, 32–43.

Brody, R. P. and Cunningham, S. M. (1968) 'Personality variables and the consumer decision process', *Journal of Marketing Research*, 5, 50–57.

Bruce, G. D. and Witt, R. E. (1976) 'Personality correlates of innovative buying behaviour', *Journal of Marketing Research*, 7, 259–60.

Bruno, A. V., Hustad, R. and Pessemeier, E. (1972) *An Integrated Examination of Media Approaches to Market Segmentation*, Lafayette, Ind.: Faculty Working Paper No. 342. Institute for Research in the Behavioural, Economic and Mangement Sciences, Krannert Graduate School of Industrial Administration, Purdue University.

Bruno, A. V. and Pessemeier, E. (1972) 'An empirical investigation of the validity of selected attitude and activity measures', *Proceedings of the Third Annual Conference of the Association for Consumer Research*, pp. 456–74.

Bryant, B. E. (1977) *American Women Today and Tomorrow*, Washington, DC: US Government Printing Office.

Bucklin, L. P. (1966) 'Testing propensities to shop', *Journal of Marketing*, 30, 22–27.

Bucklin, L. P. (1967) 'The concept of mass in intra-urban shopping', *Journal of Marketing*, 31, 37–42.

Bucklin, L. P. (1971) 'Trade area boundaries: Some issues in theory and methodology', *Journal of Marketing Research*, 8, 30–7.

Bunger, P. C. and Schott, B. (1972) 'Can private brand buyers be identified', *Journal of Marketing Research*, 9, 219–22.

Burns, A. C. and Harrison, C. (1979) 'A test of the reliability of psychographics', *Journal of Marketing Research*, 16, 32–8.

Calantone, R. J. and Sawyer, A. G. (1978) 'The stability of benefit segments', *Journal of Marketing Research*, 15, 395–404.

Carlson, M. D. (1974) 'The 1972–73 Consumer Expenditure Survey', *Monthly Labour Review*, 97, 16–23.

Carmen, J. M. (1974) 'Some generalisations and problems regarding consumer problem solving in grocery store channels', in J. N. Sheth (ed.) *Models of Buyer Behaviour*, New York: Harper & Row.

Claycamp, H. J. (1965) 'Characteristics of owners of thrift deposits in commercial and savings and loan associations', *Journal of Marketing Research*, 2, 163–70.

Cohen, J. B. (1968) 'The role of personality in consumer behaviour', in H. H. Kassarjian and T. S. Robertson (eds) *Perspectives in Consumer Behaviour*, Glenview, Ill.: Scott Foresman, pp. 220–34.

Coney, K. A. (1972) 'Dogmatism and innovation: A replication', *Journal of Marketing Research*, 9, 453–5.

Converse, P. D. (1949) 'New laws of retail gravitation', *Journal of Marketing*, 14, 339–44.

Cooper, P. (1988) 'Changing lifestyles and psychographics', Paper presented at a two-part seminar on *The Challenges Currently Facing Research*, London: International Business Communications Ltd, 10–11 November.

Corder, C. (1984) *Sociomonitor, Users Manual White*, Johannesburg: Market Research Africa.

Cornish, P. (1981) 'Social grade, household compositions and earnings', *Admap*, February, 84–6.

Cosmas, S. C. (1982) 'Life styles and consumption patterns', *Journal of Consumer Research*, 8, 453–55.

Darden, W. R. and Ashton, D. (1974) 'Psychographic profiles of patronage preference groups', *Journal of Retailing*, 50, 99–112.

Darden, W. R. and Perreault, W. D. (1976) 'Identifying interurban shoppers: Multi-product purchase patterns and segmentation profiles', *Journal of Marketing Research*, 8, 51–60.

Darden, W. R. and Reynolds, F. D. (1971) 'Shopping orientations and shopping usage rates', *Journal of Marketing Research*, 8, 505–8.

Darden, W. R. and Reynolds, F. D. (1974) 'Backward profiling of male innovators', *Journal of Marketing Research*, 11, 79–85.

Davis, B. and French, W. (1989) 'Exploring advertising usage segments among the aged', *Journal of Advertising Research*, 3, 22–30.

Day, E., Davis, B., Dove, R. and French, W. (1988) 'Reaching the senior citizen market', *Journal of Advertising Research*, 28, 23–30.

Delener, N. (1990) 'The effects of religious factors on perceived risk in durable goods purchase decisions', *Journal of Consumer Research*, 7(3), 27–37.

Demby, E. (1974) 'Psychographics and from whence it came', in W. D. Wells (ed.) *Life Style and Psychographics*, Chicago: American Marketing Association, pp. 9–30.

Derrick, F. W. and Lehfield, A. K. (1980) 'The family life cycle: An alternative approach', *Journal of Consumer Research*, 7, 214–17.

Dichter, E. (1958) 'Typology', *Motivational Publications*, 3(3), September.

Dichter, E. (1960) *The Strategy of Desire*, New York: Doubleday.

Dichter, E. (1964) *Handbook of Consumer Motivation*, New York: McGraw Hill.

Dohrenwend, B. S., Krasnoff, K., Askenasy, A. R. and Dohrenwend, B. P. (1973) 'Exemplification of a method for scaling life events: the PERI life events scale', *Journal of Health and Social Behaviour*, 19, 205–29.

Dommermuth, W. P. and Cundiff, E. W. (1967) 'Shopping goods, shopping centres and selling strategies', *Journal of Marketing*, 31, 32–6.

Domzal, T. J. and Kernan, J. B. (1983) 'Television audience segmentation according to need gratification', *Journal of Advertising Research*, 10, 37–49.

Donnelly, J. H. Jr. (1970) 'Social character and acceptance of new products', *Journal of Marketing Research*, 7, 111–13.

Dorny. L. R. (1971) 'Observations on psychographics', *Attitude Research Reaches New Heights*, Chicago: American Marketing Association, Marketing Research Series, Number 14, pp. 200–1.

Douglas, S. P. (1975) *Working Wives and Nonworking Wives: Families as a Basis for Market Segmentation*, Marketing Science Institute.

Editor and Publisher (1972) 'Working women's food buying traits revealed', 105, 62.

Ehrenberg, A. S. C. (1968) 'On methods: the factor analytic search for programme types', *Journal of Advertising Research*, 8, 55–63.

Engel, J. F., Fiorello, H. F. and Cayley, M. A. (1972) *Market Segmentation*, New York: Holt, Rinehart and Winston.

Evans, F. B. (1959) 'Psychological and objective factors in the prediction of brand choice: Ford versus Chevrolet', *Journal of Business* 32, 340–69.

Eysenck, H. J. and Eysenck, S. B. G. (1969) *Personality Structure and Measurement*, London: Routledge & Kegan Paul.

Feather, N. (1975) *Values in Education and Society*, New York: Free Press.

Fennell, G. (1975) 'Motivation research revisited', *Journal of Advertising Research*, 15, 23–8.

Ferber, R. (1979) 'Comments on paper of life cycle analysis', in W. G. Wilkie (ed.) *Advances in Consumer Research*, Vol. 6, Ann Arbor, MI: Association for Consumer Research, pp. 146–48.

Foxall, G. R. and Goldsmith, R. E. (1988) 'Personality and consumer research: Another look', *Journal of the Market Research Society*, 30, 111–25.

Frank, R. E. and Greenberg, M. G. (1980) *The Public's Use of Television*, Beverly Hills, CA: Sage.

Frank, R. E. and Greenberg, M. G. (1984) 'Interest-based segments of TV audiences', *Journal of Advertising Research*, 11, 45–54.

Frank, R. E., Massy, W. F. and Wind, Y. (1972) *Market Segmentation*,

Englewood Cliffs, NJ: Prentice-Hall.

Fritzsche, D. J. (1981) 'An analysis of energy consumption patterns by stage of family life cycle', *Journal of Marketing Research*, 28, 227–32.

Fromm, E. (1941) *Escape from Freedom*, New York: Holt, Rinehart & Winston.

Frost, W. A. K. (1969) 'The development of a technique for TV programme assessment', *Journal of the Market Research Society*, 11, 25–44.

Fry, J. N. (1971) 'Personality variables and cigarette brand choice', *Journal of Marketing Research*, 8, 298–304.

Fry, J. N. and Siller, F. H. (1970) 'A comparison of housewife decision making in two social classes', *Journal of Marketing Research*, 7, 333–8.

Furse, D. H. and Greenberg, B. A. (1975) 'Cognitive style and attitude as a market segmentation variable: A comparison', *Journal of Advertising*, 4, 39–44.

Gensch, D. H. and Ranganathan, B. (1974) 'Evaluation of television programme content for the purposes of promotional segmentation', *Journal of Marketing Research*, 11, 307–15.

Gilly, M. C. and Enis, B. M. (1982) 'Recycling the family life cycle: A proposal for redefinition', in A. Mitchell (ed.) *Advances on Consumer Research*, Vol. 9, Ann Arbor, MI: Association for Consumer Research, pp. 271–6.

Glick, I. O. and Levy, S. J. (1962) *Living with Television*, Aldine Publishing Co.

Goldsmith, E. B. and Goldsmith, R. E. (1980) 'Dogmatism and confidence as related factors in evaluation of new products, *Psychological Reports*, 47(3), 1068–70.

Goldsmith, R. (1983) 'Psychographics and new product adoption: An exploratory study', *Perceptual and Motor Skills*, 57, 1071–6.

Gollub, J. and Javitz, H. (1989) 'Six ways to age', *American Demographics*, June, 28–30, 35–56.

Goodhart, G. J., Ehrenberg, A. S. C. and Collins, M. (1975) *The Television Audience: Patterns of Viewing*, Aldershot: Saxon House.

Gotlieb, M. J. (1959) 'Segmentation by personality types', in C. H. Stockman (ed.) *Advancing Marketing Efficiency*, Chicago: American Marketing Association.

Green, P. E., Kreiger, A. M. and Schaffer, C. M. (1985) 'Quick and simple benefit segmentation', *Journal of Advertising Research*, 25, 9–15.

Green, P. E., Wind, Y. and Jain, A. K. (1972) 'A note on measurement of social–psychological belief systems', *Journal of Marketing Research*, 9, 204–8.

Greenberg, B. (1976) 'TV for children: Communicator and audience perceptions', in R. Brown (ed.) *Children and Television*, London: Collier Macmillan.

Greenberg, B., Dervin, B. and Dominick, J. (1968) 'Do people watch "television" or "programmes"?', *Journal of Broadcasting*, 12, 367–76.

Grubb, E. L. and Gathwold, H. L. (1967) 'Consumer self-concept, symbolism and market behaviour: A theoretical approach', *Journal of Marketing*, 31, 22–7.

Gunter, B. (1985) *Dimensions of Television Violence*, Aldershot: Gower.

Gunter, B. and Wober, M. (1983) 'Television viewing and public trust', *British Journal of Social Psychology*, 22, 174–6.

Guthrie, S. (1980) 'A cognitive theory of religion', *Current Anthropology*, 21, 181–203.

Gutman, J. and Mills, M. K. (1982) 'Fashion lifestyle, self-concept, shopping orientation and store patronage: An integrative analysis', *Journal of Retailing*, 58, 64–86.

Haines, G. H., Simon, L. S. and Alexis, M. (1971) 'The dynamics of commercial structure in central city areas', *Journal of Marketing*, 35, 10–18.

Haley, R. I. (1961) 'Experimental research on attitudes toward shampoos', Unpublished paper.

Haley, R. I. (1968) 'Benefit segmentation: A decision-oriented research tool', *Journal of Marketing*, 32, 30–5.

Haley, R. I. (1971) 'Beyond benefit segmentation', *Journal of Advertising Research*, 11, 3–8.

Haley, R. I. (1984a) 'Benefit segments: Backwards and forwards', *Journal of Advertising Research*, 24, 19–24.

Haley, R. I. (1984b) 'Benefit segmentation – 20 years later', *Journal of Consumer Marketing*, 1, 5–13.

Halley-Wright, A. (1988) *Cross-Cultural Consumer Characterization*, Paper issued at the Marketing Mix Conference, Johannesburg, 6 October.

Hamby, J. (1973) 'Some personality correlates of religious orientation', *Dissertation Abstracts International, Part a, Humanities and Social Sciences*, 34, 1127–8.

Harper's (1962) 'The people next door', *Harper's Magazine* and *The Atlantic*, A research report, September.

Herman, R. O. and Beik, L. L. (1963) 'Shoppers' movements outside their local retail area', *Journal of Marketing*, 32, 45–51.

Hirschmann, E. C. (1984) 'Experience seeking: A subjectivist perspective of consumption', *Journal of Business Research*, 12, 115–36.

Hirschmann, E. C. and Mills, M. K. (1979) 'Women's occupational status, innovativeness, opinion leadership and innovative communication', *Proceedings*, Southern Marketing Association Annual Conference, R. S. Franz, R. M. Hopkins and A. Toma (eds) Lafayette: South Western Louisiana University, pp. 270–5.

Holman, R. (1984) 'A values and lifestyles perspective on human behaviour', in R.E. Pitts and A.G. Woodside (eds), *Personal Values and Consumer Psychology*, Lexington, MA: Lexington.

Horney, K. (1937) *The Neurotic Personality of Our Time*, New York: Horney. Horney.

Horton, R. L. (1979) 'Some relationships between personality and consumer decision making', *Journal of Marketing REsearch*, 16, 233–46.

Huff, D. L. (1964) 'Defining and estimating a trading area', *Journal of Marketing*, 23, 34–8.

Hughes, G. D. (1978) *Marketing Management*, Reading, Mass: Addison-Wesley.

Hugstad, P., Taylor, J. W. and Bruce, G. D. (1987) 'The effects of social class and perceived risk on consumer information search', *Journal of Consumer Marketing*, 4, 41–6.

Hustad, T. P. and Pessemeier, E. A. (1973) 'Will the real consumer activist please stand up: An examination of consumers' opinions about marketing practices', *Journal of Marketing Research*, 10, 319–24.

Hustad, T. P. and Pessemeier, E. A. (1974) 'The development and application of psychographic, life style and associated activity and attitude measures', in W. D. Wells (ed.) *Life Style and Psychographics*, Chicago: American Marketing Association, pp. 31–70.

Jackson, D. N. (1967) *Manual for the Personality Research Form*, (Research Bulletin, No. 43) London, Ontario: University of Western Ontario.

Jackson, R. W., McDaniel, S. W. and Rao, C. P. (1985) 'Food shopping and preparation: Psychographic differences of working wives and housewives', *Journal of Consumer Research*, 12, 110–13.

Jacoby, J. J. (1971a) 'Personality and innovation proneness', *Journal of Marketing Research*, 8, 244–7.

Jacoby, J. J. (1971b) 'Multiple indicant approaches for studying new product adopters', *Journal of Applied Psychology* 55, 384–8.

Kahle, L. R. (ed.) (1983) *Social Values and Social Change: Adaptation to Life in America*, New York: Praeger.

Kahle, L. R. (1984) 'The values segmentation debate continues', *Marketing News*, 18, 2.

Kahle, L. R. (1986) 'The nine nations of North America and the value basis of geographic segmentation', *Journal of Marketing*, 50, 37–47.

Kahle, L. R., Beatty, S. E. and Homer, P. (1986) 'Alternative measurement approaches to consumer values: The List of Values (LOV) and Values and Life Style (VALS)', *Journal of Consumer Research*, 13, 405–9.

Kahoe, R. (1984) 'Personality and achievement correlates of intrinsic and extrinsic religious orientations', *Journal of Personality and Social Psychology*, 219, 812–8.

Kassarjian, H. H. (1971) 'Personality and consumer behaviour: A review', *Journal of Marketing Research*, 8, 409–18.

Kassarjian, H. H. (1973) 'Personality and consumer behaviour: A review', in H. H. Kassarjian and T. S. Robertson (eds) *Perspectives in Consumer Behaviour*, Glenview, Ill.: Scott, Foresman & Company.

Kassarjian, H. H. and Sheffet M. J. (1981) 'Personality and consumer behaviour: An update', in H. H. Kassarjian and T. S. Robertson (eds) *Perspectives in Consumer Behaviour*, Glenview, Ill.: Scott, Foresman & Company.

Katz, E., Blumler, J. G. And Gurevitch, M. (1974) 'Utilization of mass communication by the individual', in J. G. Blumler and E. Katz (eds) *The Uses of Mass Communications*, Beverly Hills, CA: Sage.

Keane, J. (1985) Address at Florida Atlantic University, Boca Raton, Florida, 5 April.

Kelly, G. A. (1955) *The Psychology of Personal Constructs*, Vol. 1, New York: W. W. Norton & Co.

Kernan, J. B. (1971) 'The CAD instrument in behaviourial diagnosis' *Proceedings of the Second Annual Conference of the Association for Consumer Research*, pp. 307–12.

King, C. W. (1963) 'Fashion adoption: A rebuttal to the "trickle-down theory"', in S. A. Greyser (ed.) *Toward Scientific Marketing*, Chicago: American Marketing Association, pp. 108–25.

King, C. W. and Ring, L. J. (1975) 'Retail fashion segmentation research: Development and implementation', Paper presented at the annual meeting of the Marketing Division of the Canadian Association of Administrative

Sciences, University of Alberta, 2–3 June.

King, C. W. and Sprokes, G. B. (1973) 'The explanatory efficacy of selected types of consumer profile variables in fashion change agent identification', Institute Paper No. 425, Krannert Graduate School of Industrial Administration, Purdue University.

Kinnear, T. C., Taylor, J. R. and Sadrudin, A. A. (1972) 'Socioeconomic and personality characteristics as they relate to ecologically-constructive purchasing behaviour', *Proceedings of the Third Annual Conference of the Association for Consumer Research*, pp. 34–60.

Kinnear, T. C., Taylor, J. R. and Sadrudin, A. A. (1974) 'Ecologically concerned consumers: Who are they', *Journal of Marketing Research*, 38, 20–4.

Kirsch, A. D. and Banks, S. (1962) 'Programme types defined by factor analysis', *Journal of Advertising Research*, 2, 29–31.

Klein, M. (1983) *Discover Your Real Self*, London: Hutchinson.

Kollat, D. T. and Willett, R. P. (1960) 'Customer impulse purchasing behaviour', *Journal of Marketing Research*, 1, 6–12.

Koponen, A. (1960) 'Personality characteristics of purchasers', *Journal of Advertising Research*, 1, 6–12.

Kuehn, A. A. (1963) 'Demonstration of a relationship between psychological factors and brand choice', *Journal of Business*, 36, 237–41.

Lansing, J. B. and Morgan, J. M. (1955) 'Consumer finance over the life cycle', in C. H. Clark (ed.) *Consumer Behaviour*, Vol. 2, New York: New York University Press, pp. 36–50.

Lastovicka, J. L. (1982) 'On the validation of lifestyle traits: A review and illustration', *Journal of Marketing Research*, 19, 126–38.

Lastovicka, J. L. and Joachimsthaler, E. A. (1988) 'Improving the detection of personality–behaviour relationships in consumer research', *Journal of Consumer Research*, 14, 583–7.

Lazar, W. (1963) 'Lifestyle concepts and marketing: Toward scientific marketing', *Proceedings of the American Marketing Association*, 130–9.

Lazar, W. (1985) 'Inside the mature market', *American Demographics*, March.

Lazar, W. and Wyckham, R. (1969) 'Perceptual segmentation of department store markets', *Journal of Retailing*, 3–11.

Lazarfeld, P. F. (1935) 'The Art of Asking Why', *National Marketing Review*, 1, 26–38.

Lesser, J. A. and Hughes, M. A. (1986) 'The generalizability of psychographic market segments across geographic locations', *Journal of Marketing*, 50, 18–27.

Marcus, A. S. (1965) 'Obtaining group measures from personality test scores', *Psychological Reports*, 17, 523–31.

Maslow, A. H. (1954) *Motivation and Personality*, New York: Harper & Row.

Massy, W. F., Frank, R. E. and Lodahl, T. M. (1968) *Purchasing Behaviour and Personal Attributes*, Philadelphia: University of Pennsylvania Press.

McCall, S. H. (1977) 'Meet the workwife', *Journal of Marketing*, 41, 55–65.

McConkey, C. W. and Warren, W. E. (1987) 'Psychographic and demographic profiles of state lottery ticket purchasers', *Journal of Consumer Affairs*, 21(2), 314–27.

McCrohan, K. F. (1980) 'An application of the social character construct in market segmentation', *Journal of the Market Research Society*, 22, 263–7.

McNemar, Q. (1955) *Psychological Statistics* (Second Edition), New York: John Wiley and Sons.

Mendelsohn, H. (1983) 'Using the mass media for crime prevention', Paper presented at the Annual Convention of the American Association for Public Opinion Research, Buck Hill Falls, PA, May.

Michaels, P. W. (1973) 'Life styles and magazine exposure', in B. W. Baker and H. Becker (eds) *Combined Proceedings: Marketing Education and the Real World and Dynamic Marketing in a Changing World*, Chicago: American Marketing Association, pp. 324–31.

Mischel, W. (1968) *Personality and Assessment*, New York: John Wiley and Sons.

Mischel, W. (1973) 'Toward a cognitive social learning reconceptualisation of personality', *Psychological Review*, 80, 252–83.

Mitchell, A. (1983) *The Nine American Life Styles*, New York: Warner.

Moore, C. T. and Mason, J. B. (1969) 'A research note on major retail centre patronage', *Journal of Marketing*, 33, 61–3.

Moorthy, K. S. (1984) 'Market segmentation, self-selection and product line design', *Marketing Science*, 3, 288–307.

Moschis, G. P. (1976) 'Shopping orientations and consumer uses of information', *Journal of Retailing*, 52, 61–70.

Munson, J. M. (1984) 'Personal values: Considerations on their measurement and application to five areas of research inquiry', in R. E. Pitts and A. G. Woodside (eds) *Personal Values and Consumer Psychology*, Lexington, MA: Lexington Books.

Murphy, P. E. and Staples, W. A. (1979) 'A modernized family life cycle', *Journal of Consumer Research*, 6, 12–22.

Nichols, S. Y. and Fox, K. D. (1983) 'Buying time and saving time: Strategies for managing households production', *Journal of Consumer Research*, 10, 197–208.

Noerager, J. P. (1979) 'An assessment of CAD: A personality instrument developed specially for marketing research', *Journal of Marketing Research*, 16,(1), 53–9.

Novak, T. P. and MacEvoy, B. (1990) 'On comparing alternative segmentation schemes: The List of Values (LOV) and Values and Lifestyles (VALS)', *Journal of Consumer Research*, 17, 105–9.

Nunnally, J. C. (1967) *Psychometric Theory*, New York: McGraw-Hill.

Opinion Research Corporation (1959a) *America's Tastemakers, 1 and 2*, Princeton, NJ: Opinion Research Corporation, April–June.

Opinion Research Corporation (1959b) *The Initiators*, Princeton, NJ: Opinion Research Corporation, April–June.

Palmgreen, P. and Rayburn, J. (1982) 'Gratifications sought and media exposure: An expectancy value model', *Communication Research*, 9, 561–80.

Pernica, J. (1974) 'The second generation of market segmentation studies: An audit of buying motivations', in W. D. Wells (ed.) *Lifestyle and Psychographics*, Chicago, American Marketing Association.

Pernica, J. (1975) 'Psychographics: What can go wrong', in R. C. Carhan (ed.) *Combined Proceedings of the American Marketing Association*, pp. 45–50.

Perri, M. (1990) 'Application of the List of Values alternative psychographic assessment scale', *Psychological Reports*, 66, 403–6.

Pessemeier, E. A. and Bruno, A. (1971) *An empirical investigation of the reliability and stability of activity and attitude measures*, Reprint Series No. 391, Krannert Graduate School of Industrial Administration, Purdue University.

Peterson, R. A. (1972) 'Psychographics and media exposure', *Journal of Advertising Research*, 12, 17–20.

Plummer, J. T. (1971) 'Lifestyle patterns and commercial bank credit card usage', *Journal of Marketing*, 35, 34–41.

Plummer, J. T. (1973) 'Life style and social change: Evolutionary – not revolutionary', Paper read at the 20th Annual AMA Management Seminar, Toronto.

Plummer, J. T. (1974) 'The concept and application of life style segmentation', *Journal of Marketing*, 38, 33–7.

Potter, W. J., Forrest, E., Sapolsky, B. S. and Ware, W. (1988) 'Segmenting VCR owners', *Journal of Advertising Research*, 28, 29–37.

Prasad, V. K. (1975) 'Socio-economic product risk and patronage preferences of retail shoppers', *Journal of Marketing*, 39, 42–7.

Redman, B. J. (1980) 'The impact of women's time allocation on expenditure for meals away from home and prepared foods', *American Journal of Agricultural Economics*, 62, 234–7.

Reilly, W. J. (1953) *The Law of Retail Gravitation*, New York: W. J. Reilly & Co.

Reisman, D., Glazer, N. and Denney, R. (1950) *The Lonely Crowd*, New Haven, CT: Yale University Press.

Reynolds, F. D. (1972) 'Intermarket patronage: A psychographic study of consumer outshoppers', *Journal of Marketing*, 36, 50–4.

Reynolds, F. D. (1974) 'An analysis of catalogue buying behaviour', *Journal of Marketing*, 38, 47–51.

Reynolds, F. D., Crask, M. R. and Wells, W. D. (1977) 'The modern feminine life style', *Journal of Marketing*, 41, 38–45.

Reynolds, F. D. and Darden, W. R. (1972a) 'An analysis of selected factors associated with the adoption of new products', *Mississippi Valley Journal of Business and Economics*, 8, 31–42.

Reynolds, F. D. and Darden, W. R. (1972b) 'Intermarket patronage: A psychographic study of consumer outshoppers', *Journal of Marketing*, 36, 50–4.

Reynolds, F. D. and Martin, W. S. (1974) 'A multivariate analysis of inter-market patronage: Some empirical findings', *Journal of Business Research*, 2, 193–5.

Reynolds, T. J. and Jolly, J. P. (1980) 'Measuring personal values: An evaluation of alternative methods', *Journal of Marketing Research*, 17, 531–6.

Riche, M. F. (1989) 'Psychographics for the 1990s', *American Demographics*, July, 24–6, 30–1, 53–4.

Roberts, M. L. and Wortzel, L. H. (1979) 'New life style determinants of women's food shopping behaviour', *Journal of Marketing*, 43, 28–39.

Robertson, T. S. and Myers, J. H. (1969) 'Personality correlates of opinion leadership and innovative buying behaviour', *Journal of Marketing Research*, 6, 164–8.

Rokeach, M. (1973) *The Open and Closed Mind*, New York: Basic Books.

Roper, E. (1970) *Movers and Shakers*, New York: Harper-Atlantic Sales.

Rotter, J. B. (1965) 'General expectancies for internal versus external control of reinforcement', *Psychological Monographs*, 8011, Whole No. 609.

Rousseau, D. (1990) 'Developing and testing a model of psychographic market segmentation', *South African Tydskr. Sielk*, 20(3), 184–94.

Rubin, A. (1979) 'Television use by children and adolescents', *Human Communication Research*, 5, 109–20.

Rubin, A. (1981) 'An examination of television viewing motivations', *Communication Research*, 8, 141–65.

Rubin, A. (1983) 'Television uses and gratifications: The interactions of viewing patterns and motivations', *Journal of Broadcasting*, 27, 37–51.

Rubin, A. and Rubin, R. (1982) 'Contextual age and television use', *Human Communication Research*, 8, 228–44.

Rudnick, C. and Deni, R. (1980) 'Use of the internal–external control scale to predict preferences for products', *Psychological Reports*, 47, 1193–4.

Samli, A. C. ((1975) 'Use of segmentation index to measure store loyalty', *Journal of Retailing*, 51, 53.

Satow, K. L. and Johnson, D. K. (1977) 'Will the real working woman please stand up and approach the check-out counter?', Paper presented at the Chicago Chapter, AMA Suburban Meeting.

Schaninger, C. M. and Sciglimpaglia, D. (1981) 'The influence of cognitive personality traits and demographics on consumer information acquisition', *Journal of Consumer Research*, 8(2), 208–16.

Schiffman, L. G. and Kanuk, L. L. (1980) *Consumer Behaviour* (3rd edition), Englewood Cliffs, NJ: Prentice Hall.

Sexton, D. E. (1974) 'Differences in food shopping habits by area of residence, race and income', *Journal of Retailing*, 50, 37–48.

Snyder, M. and DeBono, K. G. (1985) 'Appeals to image and claims about quality. Understanding the psychology of advertising', *Journal of Personality and Social Psychology*, 49, 586–97.

Sparks, D. C. and Tucker, W. T. (1971) 'A multivariate analysis of personality and product use', *Journal for Marketing Research*, 8, 67–70.

Stampfl, R. W. (1978) 'The consumer life cycle', *Journal of Consumer Affairs*, 12, 209–19.

Steiner, G. A. (1963) *The People Look at Television. A Study of Audience Attitudes*, New York: Alfred A Knopf.

Stephens, N. (1982) 'The effectiveness of time-compressed television advertisements with older adults', *Journal of Advertising*, 4, 48–55.

Stone, G. P. (1954) 'Observations on the social psychology of city life', *American Journal of Sociology*, 60, 36–45.

Strickland, B. R. (1978) 'Internal–external expectancies and health-related behaviours', *Journal of Consulting and Clinical Psychology*, 46, 1192–1211.

Strober, M. H. and Weinberg, C. B. (1977) 'Strategies used by working and non-working wives to reduce time pressures', *Journal of Consumer Research*, 6, 338–48.

Sturgeon, R. S. and Hamley, R. W. (1979) 'Religiosity and anxiety', *Journal of Social Psychology*, 108, 137–8.

Sullivan, H. S. (1935) *The Interpersonal Theory of Psychiatry*, New York: Norton.

Summers, J. O. (1970) 'The identity of women's clothing fashion opinion leaders', *Journal of Marketing Research*, 7, 178–85.

Taubder, E. M. (1983) 'Why do people shop?', *Journal of Marketing*, 36, 46–9.

Teel, J. E., Bearden, W. O. and Durand, R. M. (1979) 'Psychographics of radio and television audiences', *Journal of Advertising Research*, 19, 53–6.

Thompson, J. R. (1971) 'Characteristics and behaviour of outshopping consumers', *Journal of Retailing*, 47, 70–80.

Tigert, D. J. (1969) 'A taxonomy of magazine readership applied to problems in marketing strategy and media selection', *Journal of Business*, 42, 357–63.

Tigert, D. J. (1971) 'Are television audiences really different?', Paper presented at the 54th International Marketing Association meeting, San Francisco, April.

Tigert, D. J. (1974) 'Life style analysis as a basis for media selection', in W. D. Wells (ed.) *Lifestyle and Psychographics*.

Tigert, D. J., Lathrope, R. and Bleeg, M. (1971) 'The fast food franchise: Psychographic and demographic segmentation analyses', *Journal of Retailing*, 47, 81–90.

Tigert, D. J. and Wells, W. D. (1970) 'Life style correlates of age and social class', Paper presented at the First Annual Meeting of the Association for Consumer Research, Amherst.

Twedt, D. W. (1962) 'How important to marketing strategy is the "heavy user"?', *Journal of Marketing*, 26, 71–2.

Tucker, W. T. and Painter, J. J. (1961) 'Personality and product use', *Journal of Applied Psychology*, 45, 325–9.

Venkatesh, A. (1980) 'Changing roles of women – lifestyle analysis', *Journal of Consumer Research*, 6, 189–97.

Veroff, J., Douvan, E. and Kulka, R. A. (1981) *The Inner American*, New York: Basic Books.

Villani, K. E. and Lehmann, D. R. (1975) 'An examination of the stability of AIO measures', in E. M. Mazze (ed.) *Marketing: The Challenges and the Opportunities*, Chicago: American Marketing Association, pp. 484–8.

Vivabharanthy, G. and Rink, D. R. (1984) 'The elderly: Neglected business opportunities', *Journal of Consumer Marketing*, 1, 35–46.

Vitz, P. I. and Johnson, D. (1965) 'Masculinity of smokers and the masculinity of cigarette images', *Journal of Applied Psychology*, 49, 155–9.

Wagner, J. and Hanna, S. (1983) 'The effectiveness of family life cycle variables in consumer expenditure', *Journal of Consumer Research*, 10, 281–91.

Watt, J. H. and Krull, R. (1974) 'An information theory measure of television programming', *Communication Research*, 1, 44–68.

Wells, W. D. (1966) 'General personality tests and consumer behaviour', in J. W. Newman (ed.) *On Knowing the Consumer*, New York: John Wiley and Sons.

Wells, W. D. (1969) 'The rise and fall of television programme types', *Journal of Advertising Research*, 9, 21–7.

Wells, W. D. (1974) *Life Style and Psychographics*, Chicago: American Marketing Association.

Wells, W.D. (1975) 'Psychographics: a critical review', *Journal of Marketing Research*, 12, 209–29.

Wells, W. D. and Beard, A. D. (1974) 'Personality and consumer behaviour', in S. Ward and T. S. Robertson (eds) *Consumer Behaviour. Theoretical Sources*, Englewood Cliffs, NJ: Prentice Hall.

Wells, W. D. and Gubar, G. (1966) 'The life cycle concept in marketing research', *Journal of Marketing Research*, 3, 355–63.

Wells, W. D. and Tigert, D. (1971) 'Activities, interests and opinions', *Journal of Advertising Research*, 11, 27–35.

Westfall, R. (1962) 'Psychological factors in predicting product choice', *Journal of Marketing*, 36, 34–40.

Wind, Y. (1978) 'Issues and advances in segmentation research', *Journal of Marketing Research*, 15, 317–37.

Wind, Y. and Green, P. E. (1974) 'Some conceptual measurement and analytical problems in life style research', in W. D. Wells (ed.) *Life Style and Psychographics*, Chicago: American Marketing Association.

Worthing, P. M., Venkatesan, M. and Smith, S. (1973) 'Personality and product use revisited: An exploration with the personality research form', *Journal of Applied Psychology*, 57, 179–83.

Young, S. (1973) 'Research both for strategic planning and for tactical testing', *Proceedings of the 19th Annual Conference of the Advertising Research Foundation*, New York, pp. 13–16.

Yuspeh, S. (1984) 'Syndicated values/lifestyles segmentation schemes: Use them as descriptive tools, not to select targets', *AMA Marketing News*, 18, (25 May), pp. 1*ff*.

Yuspeh, S. and Fein, G. (1982) 'Can segments be born again?', *Journal of Advertising Research*, 3, 13–23.

Ziff, R. (1971) 'Psychographics for market segmentation', *Journal of Advertising Research*, 11, 3–10.

Zillmann, D. and Bryant, J. (1985) *Selective Exposure to Communication*, Hillsdale, NJ: Lawrence Erlbaum Associates.

Index